"We know Joe and Michelle William[...] save a marriage—it's Joe and Michel[...] marriages that look or feel too far gone [...]ks to this advice from Joe and Michelle. Every couple could benefit from reading about issues that, if ignored, can undermine happiness. We all need a few copies of this book on our shelves to give away to friends in need."

> —Bill and Pam Farrel
> Directors of Farrel Communications,
> Best-selling authors of *Men Are Like Waffles—
> Women Are Like Spaghetti*

"This book is highly readable and amazingly insightful. What Joe and Michelle say really works. Lives have been changed by their counsel."

> —H. Norman Wright
> Marriage and family counselor and author

"Joe and Michelle Williams have written a knowledgeable, candid guide to reconciliation between spouses. Joe and Michelle are taking the success they achieved in rescuing their marriage from divorce and are passing it on to the rest of us. Their delivery is honest, relevant, and relatable. The twelve truths they examine regarding a marriage in crisis are significant, and the discussion questions they provide at the end of each chapter for enlightenment are extremely valuable. This book speaks eloquently to the current cultural reality that is divorce and gives an alternative choice not often mentioned in today's society: reconciliation."

> —Eric and Jennifer Garcia
> Co-Founders, Association of Marriage
> and Family Ministries (AMFM)

yes,

YOUR MARRIAGE CAN BE SAVED

JOE & MICHELLE WILLIAMS

 Tyndale House Publishers, Inc., Carol Stream, IL

A Focus on the Family book published by
Tyndale House Publishers, Inc., Carol Stream, Illinois 60188

Focus on the Family and the accompanying logo and design are federally registered trademarks of Focus on the Family, Colorado Springs, CO 80995.

TYNDALE and Tyndale's quill logo are registered trademarks of Tyndale House Publishers, Inc.

All Scripture quotations, unless otherwise indicated, are taken from the *Holy Bible, New International Version*®. NIV®. Copyright © 1973, 1978, 1984 by Biblica, Inc. ™ Used by permission of Zondervan. All rights reserved worldwide (www.zondervan.com).

Scripture quotations marked (NASB) are taken from the *New American Standard Bible*®. Copyright © 1960, 1962, 1963, 1968, 1971, 1972, 1973, 1975, 1977, 1995 by The Lockman Foundation. Used by permission. (www.Lockman.org).

People's names and certain details of their stories have been changed to protect the privacy of the individuals involved.

Editors: Liz Duckworth, Gudmund Lee
Cover design by: Jennifer Ghionzoli
Cover photo © by: Masaaki Toyoura/Getty Images. All rights reserved.
Cover photo of wedding rings © by: Anastasiya Maksymenko/iStockphoto.
All rights reserved.
Author photo by: Candy Lewis

Library of Congress Cataloging-in-Publication Data
Williams, Joe, 1947-
  Yes your marriage can be saved : 12 truths for rescuing your relationship / Joe and Michelle Williams.
    p. cm.
  ISBN-13: 978-1-58997-381-7
  1. Marriage—Religious aspects—Christianity. I. Williams, Michelle, 1948- II. Title.
  BV835.W55 2007
  248.8'44—dc22

                                                  2006037379

Printed in the United States of America
6 7 8 9 10 11 / 14 13

This book is dedicated to . . .

Our children

Elicia, M'Lissa, Jason, Heather, and Mick

You survived the blending, breaking up, and reconciliation
of our family. Thank you for not giving up on us and
for gifting us (so far) with a "quiver full"
of ten beautiful grandchildren!

And

Our pastor, David Seifert, and his wife, Ruth

David, you and Ruth always believed that God could
save our marriage. Thank you for allowing a couple with a
past like ours to begin a ministry for crisis marriages, when the
popular vote in 1990 would probably have been otherwise.

⚬⚬⚬

Contents

Acknowledgments

We are grateful to everyone at Focus on the Family for their assistance in getting this book together. Thank you, Mick, who believed in the book from its conception and pitched it to Focus for us. Thank you, Larry, for giving us this opportunity. Liz and Nanci, your encouragement, ideas, suggestions, and continual support this past year have made this project such a joy! Thank you.

A special thanks to our agent, Steve Laube, for taking such good care of us. You gave us a great jump start with your writer's workshop at Mount Hermon. And to the twelve authors in that workshop who saw our first draft: thank you for your honest evaluations and input.

Thank you, Mike and Harriett McManus, for being our mentors over the years and for keeping us on our toes! Without you, we would still be using an overhead projector—and who knows what else! We hope we made you proud.

Thank you, also, to Michael and Lori Douglass, who gave us the courage to step out into full-time ministry in 1999 and who have always believed in us. We also wish to thank our board of directors—Laura, Marion, Mark, Lori, Wade, and Don—as well as our faithful monthly supporters, and our prayer chain—Laura, Karen, Jeanne, and Cheryle—you have all been the wind beneath our wings since 1999. Your support and prayers allow us to stay in full-time ministry. Thank you.

Last, thank you to the couples and individuals who have shared their hearts, stories, tears, and praises with us over the years. You know who you are, and even though we couldn't possibly have shared everyone's story in this book, you were with us in spirit as we wrote. To those whose stories we used, thank you for being willing and vulnerable enough to have your words on paper. Also, thank you for taking time out of your lives, and for joining with us in prayer for the reader who is holding this book right now.

SPECIAL ACKNOWLEDGMENTS FROM MICHELLE

Mom, God knew exactly what kind of mother I needed when He "knit me in your womb," and I am grateful that you have always believed in me. Thank you for not giving up on me during my rebellious years and always being there when I needed you. I remember the night you said, "Michelle, you are almost forty . . . is this ever going to end?" (The night I stood on your front porch, barefoot, with all the kids, at 2:30 A.M. when Joe and I separated for the last time.) I hope this book is proof that anything is possible with God! I love you.

My dad is now in heaven, but he was in my thoughts often as I wrote. Dad, thank you for admitting to me in your later years, that if you had it to do all over again, you would have made your marriage to Mom work. Thank you, also, that you and Dee put your Christian testimony on tape to play for one of our Reconciling God's Way classes in the early years of our ministry, encouraging struggling couples to press on and stay married for the sake of their children. I'm grateful that before you died you got to see (just as God promises in Joel 2:25) that He has, indeed, made up "for the years the locust have eaten."

Pam F., thank you for telling Joe and me that we needed to get our story in writing. Your words inspired the completion of our workbook in 1996, which was the catalyst God used to propel us into full-time ministry three years later. Thank you for being my first "ministry mentor" in many ways.

Jo Klein, thank you for providing such a beautiful setting to spend days away from home writing this book. Your home at Mount Hermon was like writing in heaven!

Dennis and Geni Boyer, and office staff: thank you. Dennis, thanks for loaning me your office and computer to use this past year. (By the way, your car photos are still hanging even though you told me I could remove them when I complained about the lack of "ambiance" in your office!) Maria and Jaci, I enjoyed sharing office space and coffee with you these past several months. Geni, how can I find enough words to express my gratitude to you for your support in so many ways? I hope you know that without you, this past year would have been stressful instead of exhilarating. Thank you so much!

Laura and Penny: big hugs to you both! Laura, thank you for prayers and for spending precious hours in your busy life proofing everything from the original outline to the final manuscript and helping us meet our deadline on time!

And Penny, how could I have known when we met at Mount Hermon in Steve's workshop that you would become "Jethro" in my life? Not only did you put your own book on hold in order to proof the manuscript and encourage me along the way, but you and Clint came alongside to help us do ministry. Thank you for joining us on a most amazing journey.

Joe, thank you for allowing me to spend so many hours doing what you know I love best: setting goals and meeting deadlines—and of course, writing! Thank you, also, that when I would ask you to sit at a desk and read for hours in order to get your words and input for the book, you didn't complain. (I know you would rather have been waxing your car or working outdoors!) I love you.

SPECIAL ACKNOWLEDGMENTS FROM JOE

My oldest friend, Bill Salter: Thank you for being there and helping me get through the tough years when my marriage was in crisis.

My Thursday night men's group: Thank you for your support and commitment each week, and thank you for sharing your stories and giving me a safe place to share mine.

Pastor Velton Johnson: Thank you for helping me in my education in God's Word and for giving me an opportunity to serve at Greater True Light Baptist Church.

Pastor David Seifert: Thank you for encouraging and believing in me over the years. Thanks for your support and for not giving up on our marriage.

A special thanks to my friend Bob Falkey–"B-1 Bob": You always knew what I needed and stood beside me in the tough times.

And last but not least, Michelle: Thank you for being a godly wife, mother, and grandmother, and for keeping me from spending all my time waxing my car. We make a great team! I love you.

Introduction

W hen we separated in 1987, we were angry and confused. We were also left wondering where the "church" was in our seemingly hopeless situation. Because we'd both experienced marriage and divorce in our pasts before we became committed Christians, we were determined to figure out a way to deal with our problems and avoid yet another failed marriage. We knew enough of the Bible to believe that God hates divorce (Malachi 2:16), and we wanted desperately to keep the promises we made when we renewed our marriage vows as Christians only a few months before.

During our time apart there were many resources we lacked, which only prolonged our struggle and our separation. One of the most critical things we lacked was a healthy support system of people who understood our needs. Since we were never on the same page at the same time, couples counseling, marriage retreats, and classes geared for husbands and wives to attend together never worked for us. In fact, these things only seemed to make our situation worse because of the expectations imposed on the spouse who wasn't fully willing to participate.

Another problem we encountered during our separation was that the married couples we knew couldn't relate to what we were going through. Some people tried to rescue us and fix our marriage, but that only resulted in their burnout and frustration when our marriage crises continued to escalate out of control. Others avoided us altogether because they simply didn't know what else do to. We mistakenly believed they didn't care.

Wanting desperately to be a happy couple, we tried everything to mend our marriage, but nothing worked. While our separation was lonely, painful, and embarrassing, we now understand that God was grooming us for the "ministry of reconciliation," based on 2 Corinthians 5:18. Through trial and error, and in God's perfect timing, we reconciled nearly two years later.

In 1990, shortly after our reconciliation, we knew God was calling us to help other couples in crisis and provide them with the resources we didn't have when we were separated. Seven years later our first publication was a workbook titled *Reconciling God's Way*, which was based on the challenges we faced in our marriage and separation. The workbook and leader's guide allowed us to provide classes in our community and to assist pastors worldwide to implement ministries of reconciliation in their local churches. In 1999 we cofounded the International Center for Reconciling God's Way, Inc. and went into ministry full time.

Over the years, we've talked with hundreds of couples and individuals whose marriages were in crisis, as well as the pastors and leaders trying to help these couples. While the *Reconciling God's Way* workbook served as the basic outline for helping couples to reconcile their marriage, the book you are holding in your hands presents new tools and exercises, as well as the numerous misconceptions so many people have about marriages in crisis—including the Christian community.

While it will certainly be beneficial if you and your spouse read and discuss the tools and complete the exercises in the book together, we have found that most couples are like we were when our marriage needed help: One spouse is usually more interested in working on the marriage than the other. If your husband or wife shows little or no desire in reading or utilizing the tools and exercises right now, realize that this is common and just commit to doing your part.

We are continually amazed at how God blesses the couples and individuals who persevere in the midst of a crisis marriage, and we have no doubt that He will do the same for you.

Before You Begin: Rate Your Marriage

Without discussing it with your spouse, take a moment and rate the level of your marriage.

____ **Level One**: Arguments happen, but I am committed to our marriage.

____ **Level Two**: Quarrels are left unresolved and there is a lack of intimacy in our marriage.

____ **Level Three**: In the midst of arguments, one or both of us voice threats of separation or divorce.

____ **Level Four**: At least one of us is seriously contemplating separation or divorce.

If you rated your marriage at level two or higher, your marriage is in crisis. If you rated it at a level one, are you certain your spouse would rate it the same?

We receive calls daily from distraught husbands and devastated wives whose spouses have announced they want out of the marriage. According to most of our callers, the announcement took them completely by surprise. We also receive calls from frustrated men or women who are unhappy in their marriages and want to attend couples counseling or seminars, but their spouses refuse to participate.

Regardless of the level of crisis in your marriage, you can have harmony in your home and hope for your marriage, even if your spouse is unhappy or unwilling to do his or her part. However, first you must be honest about your situation and put a plan together. We have designed the tools and exercises in this book to be implemented with a support system over a 12-week period. In preparation for the discussion time each week, underline or take notes while reading each chapter. Here are some suggestions as to how you can best benefit from the format of the book:

1. *You can read the book and implement the tools as a couple.* If your spouse is willing to participate with you, schedule a time each week that the two of you can sit down together without interruptions. Discuss the questions at the end of each chapter, as well as the tools and exercises or anything you underlined in each chapter. Don't get overly concerned if your spouse does not want to fully participate. Count it a blessing if he or she is willing, but refrain from imposing unrealistic expectations on your spouse. Give God a chance to work things out *His* way and in *His* time.

2. *Be accountable to a "support partner."* Even if you and your spouse are going through this book as a couple, it's wise for both of you to ask a same-gender friend or acquaintance who is supportive of your marriage and spiritual growth if he or she would be willing to hold you accountable and pray for you as you implement the tools and practice the exercises. Having a same-gender support partner will take pressure off you and your spouse, and provide you both with some extra accountability and prayer support. Schedule a time to meet with this person each week for the next 12 weeks and use that time to discuss the questions at the end of each chapter, as well as the ways in which the tools and exercises are working in your marriage.

3. *Read the book and implement the tools in a small group.* If your marriage is in crisis and your spouse is unwilling or unable to implement the tools in this book, meeting with a small group (as well as your support partner) will create a double portion of accountability and support for you. Try to assemble two to six people (same gender) who would like to improve their marriages and who would be willing to meet weekly to go through the discussion questions and tools in each chapter.

~❧~

We pray that you will be comforted through what we and others will share with you in the pages of this book—and that one day you will provide the same support for those who are hurting.

"Praise be to the God and Father of our Lord Jesus Christ, the Father of compassion and the God of all comfort, who comforts us in all our troubles, so that we can comfort those in any trouble with the comfort we ourselves have received from God" (2 Corinthians 1:3–4).

1

Prayer and Church Attendance Are Not Enough

Everyone who drinks of this water will thirst again; but whoever drinks of the water that I will give him shall never thirst; but the water that I will give him will become in him a well of water springing up to eternal life.

—JOHN 4:13-14, NASB

We've just celebrated our 25th year of marriage. Our five children and ten grandchildren celebrated with us. We have so much to be thankful for: the joy we feel serving side by side in ministry; the comfort of knowing that no matter how upset we might get with each other, we will never threaten separation or divorce; and, most important, the mutual love we share for one another with Christ as the center of our marriage. We are best friends and we have fun together—but it hasn't always been that way.

◈

When Michelle and I married in January 1982, neither of us thought it was necessary to seek premarital counseling. We thought the mistakes from our past marriages and divorces would equip us for dealing with anything we might encounter in our relationship. But it turned out that being a stepdad to Michelle's three daughters (two of them teenagers) was more difficult than I ever could have imagined. In fact, Michelle and I were married less than a month when we had our first big argument over parenting issues. I walked out the door of our house and into a local bar and returned home after having more than a few drinks. Neither Michelle nor I discussed the incident for fear of starting the argument all over again. Instead, we buried it—a bad habit we continued for years to come.

Soon after we married, Michelle got pregnant, and we thought having a child together might help our marriage. We were wrong. Not only did our troubles continue, but we separated for three months when our son, Mick, was less than a year old. When we got back together, we made a promise not to separate again and things seemed great between us. But our "honeymoon period" was short-lived, and soon we were right back to our same old pattern: arguing and making up, but never resolving anything. I would often go to a bar and drink too much when we argued, and this destructive cycle continued for about three years. Then, one night after going to a bar, I returned home to find that Michelle and the kids were gone. When I located them at her mom's house the next day, she said she wasn't coming home unless I moved out. I tried to get her to change her mind, but she was adamant. So, I decided to pack a few things and go to my hometown of Santa Maria, California, to stay with family and wait for Michelle to cool off so we could work on getting back together.

❧

I (Michelle) was so fed up with our arguments and Joe's drinking that I was relieved when he went to Santa Maria. I started living as if I were single again and refused to talk to him each time he called. Then, a few weeks later, I ran into an old high school friend, and she invited me to attend church with her. Joe and I had taken the kids to church a few times, but had never attended regularly. I accepted her invitation, and even though I didn't give up my "single" lifestyle, I started going to church every week.

One Sunday morning a few weeks later, the pastor invited people to the altar who wanted to receive Christ. The pastor also explained the importance of Christians who had been living outside of God's will to rededicate their lives to Him. I knew God was speaking to my heart and telling me to change my ways once and for all. Although I had prayed to receive Christ and was baptized in 1975 during a week-long Christian crusade, I never got involved in a church or studied the Bible. As a result, my relationship with the Lord didn't grow, and I continued to look for significance from the love of men rather than God. That Sunday I repented of my ways and prayed to rededicate my life to God. The woman I prayed with encouraged me to attend a weekly class on the foundations of the Christian faith.

Not long afterward, Joe called from Santa Maria. "Michelle," he said, "I miss you and the kids. I want you to sell our business and move here to Santa Maria with me."

"You've got to be kidding!" I told him. "I'll never do that. There's no way I'm going to live with you again. I know you're still drinking when you get angry, and I'm not going to walk on eggshells in my own home. If you miss the kids, then you can move back here, but I'm not moving six hours away." I concluded the conversation with the big clincher: "Besides, I've started attending church regularly, and I've found out that we are 'unequally yoked.' So, I don't have to reconcile with you."

Unequally yoked was a term someone shared with me from the passage in 2 Corinthians 6:14 about Christians not partnering with unbelievers, and I was happy to misuse it as biblical confirmation that I didn't have to reconcile with Joe. Even though I had stopped dating other men and made a recommitment to follow Jesus, I was still doing things my way rather than God's, and I was determined to live life without Joe. I enjoyed the peace in our home now that we were apart.

Joe was pretty frustrated when we hung up, but a week or so later, he came back to Modesto and moved in with one of his friends. The following Sunday he showed up at the same church I was now attending. When the pastor gave the invitation to receive Christ, Joe walked forward. *He's just trying to trick me into going back with him by pretending to become a Christian,* I thought angrily.

⤜❦⤏

I (Joe) didn't want another divorce and hoped to save our marriage by moving back to Modesto. My parents went through a bitter divorce when I was young, and my dad never modeled how to be a godly husband or father. It seemed I was following in his footsteps. When I relocated to Modesto prior to meeting Michelle, my son Jason, from my first marriage, was a teenager. After Michelle and I got married, I saw Jason only a couple of times a year and, as a result, I was not the dad he needed me to be. I knew that if I didn't start living life differently, the same thing was going to happen in my relationship with my son Mick.

When I walked forward to receive Christ that Sunday, I meant it. I made a commitment to change and I wanted to become a godly husband and father. The following week, I went to the same foundations class Michelle was attending, but that made her angry.

"Joe, this is my church! Get your own," she said one night. She even refused to use my last name and, instead, used her middle name. She also sat across the room in the foundations class and acted as if she didn't even know me. Regardless of her reactions, I continued to show up at church and attend the class. I was baptized a few weeks later.

I think Michelle finally got worn out from trying to stay mad at me. One night after class, she asked me if I would consider meeting with the pastor and his wife to discuss our marriage situation. Because she wasn't using my last name and refused to sit with me, they never connected us as husband and wife. We all had a good laugh when they realized I was the husband Michelle had been complaining about all those months. A short time later, we renewed our vows—as Christians—in front of the whole church.

Church and Prayer Produce Solid Marriages, Right?

In the fall of 1987, about eight months after we renewed our vows, I sat beside Joe as we waited for the leader of an evangelism class at our church to give us instructions. We thought that taking the class and serving God as a couple might make our marriage stronger. People at church had told us when we reconciled that as long as we prayed together, attended church as a family, and served in ministry together, we would avoid separating again.

The leader began, "Please condense your Christian testimony into a two-minute presentation for the purpose of sharing it with unbelievers. Fill in the blanks in the following sentences: *Before I was a Christian, I* _____. *And now that I am a Christian, I*_____."

As I sat in class that evening, thinking about how my life had changed since rededicating it to Christ the previous year, I came to a troubling realization: My life had not really changed that much at all. Despite our best attempts to make it appear otherwise, our marriage was, once again, in crisis. As Joe sat beside me effortlessly filling in the blanks on his paper, I wondered what in the world he could possibly be writing. Did he think we were happy just because we told people we were? Did he really think he had changed since becoming a Christian several months earlier? Hadn't he noticed that although we were regularly attending church and praying together, we still hadn't learned how to express our frustrations without deeply hurting one another? I wondered whether all the other couples in the class and in our church were as happily married behind the scenes as they seemed to appear on the outside. Or, like us, were they simply covering up a lifetime of hurts with polite smiles and hearty handshakes? (In fact, within that year, two of the couples in the class divorced, and two years later the pastor leading the class left ministry altogether because of a crisis in his marriage.)

The weeks that followed turned into a battle of wills between Joe and me.

"Joe, we need to go to counseling or to one of those weekend retreats that help couples get to the root of their marital problems," I demanded most every time we got into one of our heated arguments, which often ended without resolution.

"No, it's too expensive! Besides, we usually end up fighting over what the counselor says anyway!" he would shout back, digging his heels in even deeper.

The familiar feeling of hopelessness was beginning to return. The thought of facing a third separation was overwhelming. Because we were now both Christians, we imposed expectations on ourselves that weren't there the first two times we separated. To make matters worse, we had renewed our vows in front of the entire church only a few months earlier, and our pastor often used us as an example of how God could heal a marriage and bring hope to any situation that seemed utterly hopeless. To admit we were in crisis again meant we might cause despair for those who looked to us for hope in their own situations.

In an effort to grow closer with each other and other couples, we joined a home fellowship group. One night, the leaders of the group asked if anyone needed special prayer. Without thinking I blurted out, "Yes, we do! Joe and I are struggling again in our marriage." I felt a sense of relief as the truth came out, but what happened next took me by surprise.

We were asked to sit in the middle of the room so that everyone could pray over us. Neither of us had ever been "prayed over" before, but I was willing to try anything at that point. Everyone was so loving as they each asked God to heal and bless our marriage and to help us resolve our differences; I didn't have the heart to tell them their prayers were not working. Instead, when one of the members asked us how things were going the following week, I lied. "Thank you so much for praying over us. Yes, your prayers worked and things are so much better between us."

～☙～

I was as frustrated as Michelle when our marriage troubles resurfaced. From the start of our marriage, we fought over everything: money, parenting, my family, her family—you name it, we fought about it. Our natural tendencies of dealing with conflict only made matters worse.

I tended to stuff what I really felt and during the years leading up to the renewal of our vows, I would lose control with the aid of alcohol. Michelle could take it for only so long before she would explode in rage when keeping the peace in our home became more than she could handle. I had expected things to change after we became Christians and renewed our vows in the church, especially because I'd stopped drinking. But when our arguments started escalating again a few months later, it was hard to know where to turn.

Finally, Michelle convinced me to go with her for a weekly counseling appointment with one of the pastors at our church. But unfortunately, after the third week of counseling we started fighting over new things: what one of us said or didn't say during the session; whether or not we completed the assignment the pastor gave us; or even whose side the pastor was on regarding issues we brought up during the appointment!

I finally told Michelle I wasn't going back. Refusing to attend definitely didn't help our situation. One night during an argument, I packed my bags and left. I wanted to visit my family in Santa Maria and take a break from all the fighting.

When I took off that night, I didn't intend for our separation to be permanent. But when I tried to go back home a couple of weeks later, Michelle said the only way she would let me stay was if we went into counseling again. I didn't want to do that. Since neither of us would back down, I decided to get an apartment. I figured we would settle our differences in a month or two, once we both cooled off.

I had no idea it would take two years.

~⊚~

While it is true that attending church and praying together are good for couples, it is a misconception that doing so will prevent separation or divorce. The truth is that churches across America are filled with couples who have made a commitment to Christ, attend church and pray together, and whose marriages are in crisis. If you have made a commitment to Jesus and consider yourself a Christian, there is no guarantee that your marriage will be crisis free. However, if you will allow Jesus to walk beside you during your crisis, He will provide everything you need to get through it.

The Well of "Living Water"

In John chapter 4, Jesus addressed a woman at a well in Samaria. She had been married five times and was living with her lover. Jesus drew her to Himself during their conversation because He knew she was trying to fill the emptiness in her life with love from men rather than God. Jesus promised to give her His living water, and she left the well that day never thirsting for love again.

Because of our pasts, the pastor who helped us renew our vows lovingly refers to us as "the man *and* the woman at the well." But the Samaritan woman's story is applicable to all of us. Jesus wants to draw everyone to a place where they will come to Him to satisfy their thirst with the Holy Spirit. In spite of different pasts and experiences, we all share a common thirst that entices us to the well of living water. Why some choose to drink and others walk away is a mystery to us, but we know that Jesus brings everyone to His well—His way. Could God be bringing you to the well through a crisis in your marriage?

Group or Support-Partner Discussion Questions

1. *Were you raised in a home with religious values? How did that shape who you are today?*
2. *Did you have a good relationship with your parents while growing up? What about now?*
3. *Did your parents model a good marriage? Explain.*
4. *How do you tend to handle stress in a crisis situation?*
5. *Look up and discuss John 14:1-3.*
6. *What is one thing that you are grateful for in your spouse?*
7. *What is one thing that you need prayer for?*

You Need to Build a Safe Support System

For where two or three have gathered together in My name, I am there in their midst.

—MATTHEW 18:20, NASB

*T*he morning after Joe moved out, I showed up alone for our weekly counseling appointment with the pastor. I could tell he was disappointed that Joe and I had separated again, but he did his best to try to encourage me and give sound advice. "Michelle, you need to do everything you can to be a godly wife, regardless of whether or not your husband is living at home. Don't focus on what Joe is doing—just do your part."

For someone who had spent the majority of her life going from one dysfunctional marriage to another, that was going to be hard advice to follow. *How can I be a godly wife without a husband in the home? And, who will be there for me now that Joe is gone?* I wondered. My apprehension must have been apparent, because the pastor's homework assignment was to study the characteristics of the godly wife in Proverbs 31.

Leaving his office that day, I felt alone and ashamed about being separated again. It was going to be so difficult to face the people who had been praying for us and who were supportive when we renewed our vows only eight months earlier.

A couple of days later, I contracted a case of the flu. Instead of praying that God would bring a quick recovery as I normally would have, I welcomed the opportunity to stay home so I could avoid having to face everyone at church. Since everything Joe and I did at church included being with other couples, I was struggling to figure out where I would fit in without him. The pastor's words about being a godly wife even though Joe wasn't in the home were still ringing in my ears.

FINDING OUR PLACES

I turned 40 while in bed with the flu. I decided that when I recovered I would join a Sunday school class geared for people 40 years of age and older. It wasn't awkward to attend that class without Joe, since it consisted mostly of senior citizens and a few widowed ladies I could sit with.

Looking back, I see that God provided me with exactly what I needed, even though it wasn't what I wanted. Although I enjoyed the Sunday school class and many of the people I met are still in my life today, I was disappointed in the pastors at our church. I had an expectation that they should supply much of my emotional support when Joe left, and that just wasn't happening. I placed countless calls to our senior pastor's administrative assistant, wanting her to tell the pastor to drop everything and meet with me each time Joe and I had an argument. Once, I even wrote our pastor an admonishing letter saying, "You renewed our vows in front of the whole church, and you always smiled and shook our hands when you saw us. Now that we aren't a 'happy couple' anymore, it seems like you are ignoring me. If I'm feeling this way, maybe there are others who feel this way too. Our pastors need to reach out and let hurting people know they care!"

The letter was written during one of those cathartic exercises; it should never have been mailed. The minute it was sent, I regretted doing so. I called the pastor's assistant to ask if she could intercept the letter when it arrived and she said she would try.

Two days later, I received a call from my pastor. He had received the letter. Thankfully, he was very gracious and the outcome of the letter actually was a behind-the-scenes ministry that I spearheaded with three other women. Our responsibility was to write notes and send cards to people who were facing a crisis in their lives. It gave me great comfort to write encouraging words to people who were hurting, since I was hurting too.

❦

The only thing that saved me from losing all hope when Michelle refused to let me move back home after our last separation was my support system, which I believe was a gift from God. I mistakenly believed the pastors at our church had chosen to side with Michelle after we separated. Out of frustration, I decided to start attending a smaller church across town. This new church offered a men's Bible study, and one of the guys invited me to attend. I had never been in a men's group and had no idea of the impact it would have on me. Not only did I learn a lot about the Bible, but I also learned to openly share my feelings with other men. I realized all of us had similar struggles—even those men who were in good marriages.

One thing I've noticed over the years since then is that most men in crisis marriages have never had a good relationship with their fathers, and few have solid male Christian role models. The men's Bible study filled a void I didn't even know I had. Even though I left our church over a misunderstanding, God used my departure to create a support system that helped me focus on Him during a very lonely time. It also gave me an opportunity to spend time with other Christian men who were mature in their walks with the Lord.

Michelle and I realize now that our pastors could not have given us everything we needed when we separated, but that doesn't lessen the pain we felt. Separation is hard—sometimes I think even more difficult than divorce or death because you aren't single, but you don't feel married anymore either. And, as a Christian, separation is worse because you sit in church and watch other couples and families interact with each other.

We continually get calls from people who are going through a separation or divorce and have left their church because they felt abandoned by their pastors during their crisis. But that's the Enemy's way of isolating the person in crisis and making him or her feel that pastors don't care. The truth is, most pastors do care—they just can't do it all. We get almost as many calls from pastors and people wanting to start reconciliation ministries as we do from couples whose marriages are in crisis. It is a misconception that pastors are the only ones who are responsible to help when someone in their church is in crisis.

The Bible is full of examples of the ways in which God expects His people to care for one another, and no where does He state that pastors are the ones who are supposed to do it all. In fact, in several passages God encourages quite the opposite. For instance, when Moses tried desperately to mediate all the Israelites' disputes while they were wandering in the desert, his father-in-law recognized the impossible situation. "What you are doing is not good," he told Moses. "You and these people who come to you will only wear yourselves out. The work is too heavy for you; you cannot handle it alone." (Exodus 18:17-18). Jethro told Moses to select capable men to assist him, men who feared God and loved the truth.

With the high divorce rate among Christians today, pastors need help as desperately as Moses did. And that help needs to come from others in the church. That's why support partners and small groups are so important.

Steps to Building a Safe Support System

If you are going through a lonely time because your spouse isn't there for you right now, we know how you feel and want to help you get the support you need. Since we didn't reconcile for almost two years, our support systems became our lifelines. We are convinced that without godly support and accountability, we would not have stayed committed to God, and certainly not each other.

A safe support system is one that helps you grow closer to God and stay focused on Him—*regardless of your circumstances*. A word of caution is appropriate here: Be careful not to seek support from someone of the opposite gender. Protect your emotions and the emotions of those around you. At least half of the people we talk with whose marriages are in crisis say they or their spouses are involved in adulterous relationships that began as "innocent" friendships. You are in a vulnerable place right now, and the next step you take needs to be one that draws you closer to God.

1. Build a prayer team. Prayer is a key part of your support system—especially if your spouse is unwilling to work on the marriage with you. However, don't expect all your prayer support to come from just one person or else you will run the risk of wearing out your welcome. Proverbs 25:17 says, "Seldom set foot in your neighbor's house—too much of you, and he will hate you." Strong words, but true when it comes to placing unrealistic expectations on others. Build a same-gender prayer team of three to five people in order to spread out your phone calls and prayer requests.

2. Find a same-gender support partner. It is vital that you have someone to walk alongside you if your marriage is in crisis. My best friend from high school was my support partner during my separation from Joe. Karin prayed for our marriage and helped me stay focused on God. Neither of us knew a lot about the Bible, but we searched the Scriptures together and asked our pastors and leaders lots of questions. As a result, we helped each other grow spiritually. A word of caution here: Just as Moses was instructed to look for special qualities when choosing people to help him, your support partner should exhibit these three qualities:

1. A healthy fear of God (Proverbs 1:7)
2. A steadfast love for the truth of God's Word (Proverbs 2:1-5)
3. A willingness to regularly pray for your marriage (1 Peter 4:7-8)

~❦~

Your support partner doesn't have to know the Bible in-depth, nor does he or she have to attend your church. Many individuals have found their support partners at work. One man shared this about how he found his support partner: "I didn't know anyone at my church or workplace who could be my support partner, so I waited and prayed about it for three weeks. One day, I felt that God wanted me to ask this older man at church if he would be my support partner. I approached him and said, 'My marriage is in crisis, and I'm taking a class on reconciliation. I'm supposed to ask someone to be my support partner and I was wondering if you would consider meeting with me each week to go through a workbook?'

"The man's eyes filled with tears! When I asked him if I'd said something wrong, he replied, 'No, you haven't said anything wrong. You've said everything right. I've been attending church for a long time and never felt worthy of serving anywhere. This is the first time I've felt as if I might be able to help someone else.' "

This man's comments are typical of many people who sit in our pews every week and never think God can use them. When you step out to ask someone to be your support partner, you not only help yourself and take pressure off the pastors and leaders to do it all, you also give someone else an opportunity to feel needed.

3. Attend a same-gender support group. Most communities offer a variety of faith-based support groups that deal with specific needs. Find a support group that centers on Christian principles. If your church doesn't offer anything, contact one of the larger Christian churches in your area. In their book *Safe People*, psychologists Henry Cloud and John Townsend speak about an important aspect of support groups: "A dynamic occurs in a group that is absent in one-on-one relationships. Members realize the universality of pain and suffering, and they are not as tempted to condemn themselves."[1]

Mary is an example of someone who found the comfort she needed in a same-gender support group after her husband walked out: "When I realized my husband had been unfaithful, I was devastated. The words *separation* and *divorce* weren't even part of my vocabulary. I was a Christian—active in our church—and I believed and trusted God for direction in my life. When my husband said he was leaving me, I panicked and didn't know where to turn. I was embarrassed and hurt, and all I could think about was saving my marriage.

"At first I was hesitant to go to our church leaders because I was teaching in a Christian school and was afraid of losing my job. Instead, I contacted a ministry outside our church for advice. Through this ministry, I was able to find a Christian women's support group about 15 miles from home.

"I continued to attend our church and, although many people at my church were supportive, I still had a difficult time because that was where I felt the loneliest. I was constantly reminded of the life I knew with my husband and children when we were a family together. The other families there looked so happy while I was hurting on the inside.

I continued to attend the weekly support group outside my church. With the group's help, I learned to take my focus off trying to save my marriage and put it on trusting God to do what was best.

"My prayer group, which consisted of seven ladies—some from my church—was also an important part of my support system. When my husband first left me, one of the ladies called me every morning just to make sure I was up and ready to go to work. Another allowed me to call her late at night if I needed to, which was very helpful. That was sometimes the hardest and loneliest part of the day. God seemed to work it out so that I had contact with one of these ladies every day. I could never have gone through my marriage crisis without my weekly support group and their prayers."

4. *Attend a group Bible study.* Attending a Bible study offers you an opportunity to meet other people who are spiritually mature. The discussion times will help you grow in your relationship with the Lord and with others. Choose a Bible study in which the leaders have been trained to teach solid doctrine. The apostle Paul wrote to Titus, "You must teach what is in accord with sound doctrine. Teach the older men to be temperate, worthy of respect, self-controlled, and sound in faith, in love and in endurance. Likewise, teach the older women to be reverent in the way they live, not to be slanderers or addicted to much wine, but to teach what is good" (Titus 2:1-3).

5. *Be discipled by a mature Christian (especially if you are a new believer).* In your church or Bible study, find someone who is more spiritually mature than you. This person needs to know Scripture well enough to help you stay on track biblically. When Joe and I were separated, I was discipled by two women. After I read about the importance of older women teaching younger women (see Titus 2:3-5), I asked a retired school teacher from my Sunday school class if she would be willing to disciple me. Leah and I met every Friday morning. Instead of going through a structured study, I asked her for advice

in particular situations—either with Joe, the kids, or my work. She would usually say, "Well, I'm not sure what you should do, but let's go to God's Word and see what *He* thinks you should do." It was a great way for me to learn how to find biblically-based answers for daily living.

The other woman who discipled me was about my age, but she had been a Christian and studied the Bible longer than I had. Sally and I lived near each other and walked together every morning for exercise. She lovingly confronted me every time I took Scripture out of context to get my way—which was more often than I'd like to admit.

Guard Your Heart

Having a safe support system if your spouse isn't there for you will help you avoid making many of the same mistakes we and others have made. But you will also have to take extra precautions to guard your heart when you are feeling lonely. Here are some steps that can help:

1. Avoid thinking of yourself as single. Look at your ring finger on your left hand right now. Are you wearing a wedding ring? I (Joe) do a "ring check" almost every week with my Thursday night men's group. I remind the guys whose marriages are in crisis that they are still married—even if their spouses have filed for divorce. If you start thinking you are single because your spouse isn't working on the marriage or has filed for divorce, you're believing a lie, and it isn't from God. It doesn't matter how hopeless things may look. Stay focused on God, wear your wedding band, and keep your heart prepared to reconcile with your spouse. Until your spouse dies or remarries, God's best is for you to be content in your circumstances so He can work a miracle.

In the next chapter you will read about couples whose marriages were saved, even though reconciling with one another looked impossible.

2. Avoid going to a single's ministry if you are still married. Some churches have active single's ministries that offer an array of wonderful programs. However, if you are still married or recently divorced and still vulnerable, it is best to avoid social settings that could lead to an emotional or physical bond that might prevent reconciliation with your spouse.

3. Avoid spouse bashing. Some support groups overly focus on the negative behaviors of spouses. Naturally, if domestic violence or severe verbal abuse is present, it is important not to deny the offense (more on this issue in chapter 8). However, a healthy support group will help you make positive changes rather than focus on what your spouse is doing wrong. If you find that the people in your group are spending the majority of their time discussing the shortcomings of their spouses, it is probably time to move on and find a healthier group.

4. Avoid dropping your support system once your crisis is over. We pray that your marriage will become a relationship that glorifies God. However, don't do what so many people do once they reconcile with their spouses: They drop their support system. We have watched people fall from the mountaintop of reconciliation to the pit of deep despair because their focus shifted back to their spouses and their problems. Without their support system in place, they stopped doing all the things that initially helped them shift their focus to God.

LIVING LIFE GOD'S WAY—EVEN WITH AN UNWILLING SPOUSE

Once your support system is in place, Jesus will use this team to love and encourage you through His Word and help you make wise decisions (we discuss this more in depth in chapter 10). We often hear people say, "That person is Jesus with skin on," when they talk about a Christian brother or sister who has come alongside them during a crisis.

In addition to creating your support team, you may also need to make some changes in your personal life. Here are four steps to take:

1. Evaluate your friendships. Many of the couples we receive calls from tell us that they or their spouses have struggled with third-party involvement. This happens in ministry settings as well as in the workplace. If you already have an emotional and/or physical bond with someone other than your spouse, you must break off that relationship if you want to begin making wise choices for your marriage. This may even include a same-gender friend who is not supportive of your spouse or who tempts you to spend too much time away from home.

2. Evaluate your family time. When a marriage is in crisis, instead of spending more time at home with family, people tend to become involved in excessive work or play away from the home. Ask your spouse and your children if your life is in balance in this area—they will usually be the first to tell you the truth.

Some women have realized they need to give up a hobby or ministry, or quit working so many hours away from home in order to spend more time with their families. Some men have realized they've focused on work to the point where they provided and provided until they divided and lost their families. Of course, on the other end of the spectrum, there are also men who have admitted they lost their families because they refused to work at all.

3. Evaluate the atmosphere in your home. Regardless of your gender or role in the home, do whatever you can to get your home in order and make it an inviting place for your family. Sometimes simple tasks such as rearranging the furniture, getting new sheets, working in the yard, or adding a coat of paint to the walls will be enough to change negative moods into positive ones. Many people with whom we have shared this tool say it alone helped to open up positive communication with an unhappy spouse.

4. Evaluate your health. When a marriage is in crisis, stress levels elevate, which can cause health challenges. Consequently, extra precautions are needed during this time. If you haven't been eating right, exercising, or taking care of your health, start now. Start slowly and set some short-term, measurable goals. Celebrate each day when you meet your goals and move forward to the next ones.

SOMETIMES IT'S OKAY TO FEEL LONELY

Staying connected to others through a safe support system will help you get through your marriage crisis God's way, but don't make the mistake of thinking you must fill every waking moment with people and activities to avoid being lonely. We both struggled in this area. As young adults we discovered the feeling of "falling in love" was a great antidote to loneliness. That's why we were so drawn to each other. We were together all the time until we married only six months later. The adrenaline high of first falling in love—or getting back together after a separation—can be as intoxicating as getting high on drugs or alcohol. Even after we became Christians, we struggled in the area of loneliness.

What neither of us understood was that the loneliness we were feeling was really for God and not other people. People try to fill this hole with worldly things such as love outside of marriage, lustful sex, drugs, excessive shopping, overeating, and so on. That's why the apostle John warned the early Christians to guard against anything that might take their focus off God: "For everything in the world—the cravings of sinful man, the lust of his eyes and the boasting of what he has and does—comes not from the Father but from the world. The world and its desires pass away, but the man who does the will of God lives forever" (1 John 2:16-17).

~ତ~

What is your greatest struggle right now? Do you feel abandoned by your spouse or others or both? You might even feel abandoned by God because many of your prayers seem unanswered. We know how you feel because we were once there too. Don't lose heart. Every person we know who stayed focused on God when their marriages and families were in crisis has come through their crises feeling closer to God and their spouses. In the next chapter you will meet some of these people and learn how to wait for God's answers.

Group or Support-Partner Discussion Questions

1. *Are you connected with a local church? What support structures does your church have that you can tap into?*

2. *Why is same-gender support important? When you think of possible same-gender support partners, who comes to mind? Why?*

3. *Discuss the value of a safe support system when a marriage is in crisis.*

4. *What do you feel your immediate responsibility is in your particular situation?*

5. *Look up and discuss 1 John 4:11-13.*

6. *What is something you are thankful for this week?*

7. *What is your greatest concern? Ask your spouse, support partner, or small group to pray for you this week. Ask how you can pray for them as well.*

3

God Will Answer Your Prayers, His Way

Behold, I stand at the door and knock; if anyone hears My
voice and opens the door, I will come in to him and will
dine with him, and he with Me.

—REVELATION 3:20, NASB

*M*ost of the couples and individuals who contact us admit that they have prayed to God for clear direction but feel confused because their marriage troubles continue. Clint and Penny were married less than two years and had just returned from a mission trip when Penny made the decision to end their marriage. "Don't get me wrong," she wrote in her book *The Path of Most Resistance*.[1] "When I left Clint, I didn't stop believing in God for a moment. I just stopped communicating with Him." When Penny moved out, Clint went to the elders of their church and asked for prayer. Every Sunday after church for six weeks they all prayed and believed that Penny would repent and stop the divorce. Clint continued to pray, trusting that God would heal their marriage, but the divorce became final. Finally, when all hope of reconciling with Penny vanished, Clint decided to leave California to begin a new life in Florida.

Eleven years went by. One day Clint received a letter from Penny, who was living 3,000 miles away. She had repented and reconciled with God. She sensed God was prompting her to ask Clint's forgiveness for ending their marriage. When he received Penny's letter, he called her and they talked on the phone for five hours. Neither had remarried and they decided to meet face-to-face and discuss the issues that led up to Penny walking out on their marriage.

In a letter written and mailed to Penny the day after their long phone conversation, Clint wrote, "I forgave you years ago, but like I told you last night, it has only been in the last few months that I asked the Lord to forgive me for being secretly angry at Him for our breakup. He answered my prayers last night with you on the phone. I have peace now. Thank you."[2]

After 11 years of silence, God answered Clint's prayers. He and Penny remarried a few months later. Today, Clint and Penny serve in ministry together in Dublin, California,[3] and also partner with us in our national reconciliation focus group helping couples reconcile their marriages.

Earl and Kaye are another couple whose prayers God answered after years of silence. They were married the first time in 1969, but in the first month of their marriage Kaye was raped and left for dead. Although Kaye survived, their young marriage didn't. "We went our separate ways, but in the back of our hearts, we never forgot each other." Thirty-five years later they remarried! They also serve in ministry together in Chico, California,[4] helping couples reconcile.

There's no doubt that God can work miracles in your marriage, and you should continue asking and believing that He will. But it is a misconception to think that He will heal your marriage just because you've asked. Scriptures such as James 1:5-6 instruct us to ask God, believe, and not doubt. But James also warns us not to be overly confident: "Instead, you ought to say, 'If it is the Lord's will, we will live and do this or that.' As it is, you boast and brag. All such boasting is evil" (James 4:15-16).

The late J. Vernon McGee, author and Bible scholar, commented on the subject of God always giving us what we pray for: "It is pious nonsense to think you can force God to do something (and) that God has to do it because you believe it. I have made it through a number of years now with cancer in my body, and no one wants to be healed more than I do. Don't tell me that I don't believe in faith healing—I do. However, I have been told that I can force God, that God *will* heal me if I demand it. I don't know what His will is, but whatever His will is, that is what I want done. God wants us to bring our needs to Him, but He has to be the one to determine how He will answer our prayers."[5]

WATCH FOR GOD'S ANSWERS

The problem with expecting God to answer your prayers the way you think He should is that if you are looking for one specific answer, you just might miss His answer altogether. I (Michelle) get calls regularly from Christian women whose non-Christian husbands have left and filed for divorce. Many feel abandoned by God because they asked Him to save their marriages, and instead, their spouses married someone else. In many of these cases, their husbands were committing adultery and/or were physically abusive. But because they expected God's answer to come in the form of a saved marriage, these women missed the fact that God answered their prayers by releasing them from abusive or unhealthy marriages.

Read what Paul said in 1 Corinthians 7:15: "But if the unbeliever leaves, let him do so. A believing man or woman is not bound in such circumstances; God has called us to live in peace." (Read all of 1 Corinthians 7 when you have time in order to get the whole context of Paul's message in these verses.)

After being in ministry for so many years, we have learned that

God answers prayers in His own time and in His own way. The important thing is to trust Him to give you the answer you need, even though it may not be the answer you want.

Kathy's roller-coaster marriage was taking a toll. She and her husband had just separated again for the eighth time when she decided to enroll in a reconciliation class at her church. She faithfully attended the 12-week class, praying that her husband would join her, but he never did. When the class was over, she joined a support group and Bible study for women whose marriages were in crisis. Kathy held on to the hope that her marriage would be saved, and she prayed daily for her husband. Still, he refused to move back home.

"When I told my husband that I would do whatever it took to save our marriage, he told me that he was filing for divorce. I cried a lot at first and wasn't motivated to do anything. I had dropped to one hundred pounds and had to force myself to eat. This is what I wrote in my journal during that time: 'This is the Lord's battle, and I will recruit prayer warriors to help! I only hope this is a short battle.' Soon after that entry, the Lord led me to the support group for women whose marriages were in crisis."

Although Kathy prayed for her husband daily and trusted God to work a miracle in her marriage, it ended in an unwanted divorce. A couple years later, Kathy married Don, a wonderful Christian man. They dated for a while and when they felt ready, took several classes in order to prepare for their marriage. Four years later, Don and Kathy started a ministry for blended families in Riverbank, California.[6] Even though Kathy's first marriage ended, God blessed her desire to do things His way, and today she and Don are using the pain from their pasts to help couples prepare for and adjust to remarriage and step-family challenges.

In some cases, instead of changing stressful circumstances, God gives us the grace to live with them, as in Richard's case. When I (Joe) first spoke to Richard about his crisis marriage, I knew he would need a lot of prayer and support. Richard, his wife, and their four children lived on the East Coast. His wife had just been diagnosed with a mental disorder. She claimed she didn't love him anymore and that God was telling her to divorce him. I recommended he get a support partner and a prayer team together, and that he join a men's group as soon as possible. I agreed to be part of his support system in terms of prayer and phone calls. He admitted he wasn't very mature in his Christian faith, so I encouraged him to find a good Bible-teaching church and someone to disciple him.

Richard was desperate to save his marriage and have his wife healed. We kept in touch over the next several months. One time he asked, "Why is God letting this happen to our family? I am praying and asking Him to heal her, and yet things are getting worse." At one point his wife ended up in a mental facility and wouldn't even let him visit her. I told him to just keep doing his part and keep his focus on God and eventually he would have answers to his questions.

Several months later, with the help of medication, Richard's wife was able to move back home. Richard called me one evening, ecstatic that God had saved his marriage and that his wife was healed. I rejoiced with him but cautioned him not to drop his support system. He agreed to continue attending his men's group, staying focused on God, and calling me as needed. It seemed that God had answered Richard's prayers and that his wife had truly been healed. But things took a turn for the worse the following year.

Richard's wife decided to stop taking her medication a year after they reconciled. Thankfully, he had continued to keep his support system intact and was able to face his crisis with a strong faith in the Lord. That was almost five years ago, and his wife still struggles with depression. He has accepted the fact that their marriage will probably always be difficult, but he is committed to staying faithful to her and keeping his focus on God. He keeps in regular contact with his support partner and still calls me every so often. Not long ago he said, "I know that if my marriage hadn't been in crisis, my walk with the Lord wouldn't be as strong as it is, so I'm okay with having a marriage that is less than perfect. My relationship with God and with my children has helped me to feel joyful even though my wife hasn't been healed."

GOD'S SILENCE MEANS "WAIT"

At times God seems silent. Most of us have heard the saying: "God always answers prayer. Sometimes He says yes, sometimes He says no, and sometimes He says wait." Unlike Richard, many people who are waiting think that God's silence means He either can't hear their prayers or He doesn't care. According to author and seminary teacher Oswald Chambers, God's silence actually means the opposite:

> God's silences are His answers. . . . His silence is the sign that He is bringing you into a marvelous understanding of Himself. Are you mourning before God because you have not had an audible response? You will find that God has trusted you in the most intimate way possible, with an absolute silence, not of despair, but of pleasure, because He saw that you could stand a bigger revelation. . . . A wonderful thing about God's silence is that the contagion of His stillness gets into you and you become perfectly confident—"I know God has heard me." His silence is proof that He has. . . . If Jesus Christ is bringing you into the understanding that prayer is for the glorifying of His Father, He will give you the first sign of His intimacy—silence.[7]

Several weeks prior to our reconciliation, Joe came to the house one day and tried to convince me that we needed to move back in together. He almost seemed demanding: "Michelle, we are living outside of God's will, and you need to let me move back home now." I was confused because we were still fighting so much and there was an element of love and concern missing in Joe's desire to reconcile. I wanted to do God's will and was praying for a clear answer, but it seemed that God was silent. I didn't understand at the time that God was actually telling me to "wait." That silent time resulted in one of the most beautiful experiences with God that I have ever had.

One day during this period, I decided to go away and spend time alone in prayer. While praying I remembered several areas of conflict in our marriage that had never been resolved. In the past when I had tried to bring them up, Joe would shut down. I counted the areas and there were six. All at once, I realized God had finally broken His silence by showing me these specific areas. "Father," I prayed, "thank You for bringing to my mind these six areas of conflict that Joe and I have never been able to discuss or resolve. I know it is Your will that we resolve them so we can reconcile and have a marriage that honors You. Lord, I will put these six issues in Your hands and trust that when they are resolved, it is Your sign that we should move back together."

After praying that prayer I had peace in my heart, trusting God to work out our reconciliation in His time. A few weeks later all six issues were discussed and settled—and Joe was the one who brought them up! To everyone's amazement we moved back in together shortly afterward.

Looking back, I am grateful that I continued to pray and spend time in God's Word while He was silent. If I had believed that God wasn't listening or didn't care, I doubt Joe and I would have ever reconciled. The list I made while crying out to God during His silence was the very thing He used to confirm it was time for us to reconcile.

Over the years Joe and I have heard couples and individuals say over and over again how they could see God's hand in their lives in times that He seemed silent. In most cases, couples whose marriages have been reconciled admit that they were tempted to throw in the towel because they got tired of waiting for God to show them answers. Karin almost did.

After years of waiting for God to heal her crisis marriage, Karin could not understand why her prayers were going unanswered. "I wish God would just give me skywriting and make it clear what I should do. I feel like He's been silent for so long!" she told me in frustration one day. Just as Karin thought all hope for their marriage was gone and that years of silence meant God was saying no, a miracle happened. Her husband had decided to move out and file for divorce, and in the process, they scheduled a meeting to divide their assets and discuss their divorce. Karin refers to that day as the day their marriage was healed. "When my husband came to our house so we could decide how to divide everything, he volunteered to come over once a week to take care of the yard so I wouldn't have to hire someone. I told him that since he would be there doing the yard, he could bring his laundry and I would do it so he wouldn't have laundry expenses. One thing led to another, and pretty soon we were communicating with soft hearts and our anger was gone! He never even moved into his apartment."

That happened more than 10 years ago and today Karin and her husband have a strong marriage and enjoy their grown children and grandchildren. What Karin didn't realize during the years that God seemed silent was that He was doing work behind the scenes that she couldn't see, in preparation for the day their hearts would be softened.

WHAT TO DO WHEN GOD SEEMS SILENT

If God seems silent in your life right now, don't lose hope. It's not easy, but if you stay focused on God and hang on to His promises during such times, the blessing that awaits you will be worth it all. Here are some guidelines that we and others have found that can help you stay focused on God while waiting for His answer:

1. *Repent of any known sin in your life so you can hear God.* Some of us get so focused on what our spouses are or aren't doing, that we neglect to deal with our own sin. Once I (Michelle) was upset with Joe because we were running late for church, and he decided to stop and put gas in the car, even though it seemed there was enough to get us there. When he didn't take my advice about waiting, I sulked. While he was filling the tank, I said to God, "Lord, why does he not listen sometimes when it's so obvious that I'm right? Things like this are so frustrating! He should have waited and filled the tank *after* church, not now." Sitting with my arms folded, tapping my foot, I happened to catch a glimpse of my sour expression in the side mirror. At once, I was convicted and even embarrassed. Here we were on our way to church (to teach a reconciliation class, no less!) and I actually thought God would be on my side because getting to church on time was so much more important than being respectful to my husband, regardless of whether he listened to my advice.

As simple as that example is, had I not repented and apologized to Joe for my attitude, that situation could have been the beginning of many other unconfessed episodes, and we know from experience that this is how layers of resentment build upon one another.

The apostle John wrote: "If we claim to be without sin, we deceive ourselves and the truth is not in us. If we confess our sins, he is faithful and just to forgive us our sins and purify us from all unrighteousness" (1 John 1:8-9). John wanted Christians to understand the importance of feeling secure with their salvation. He wasn't saying if we forget to confess or die before we can confess, we will lose our salvation. If you have confessed to God that you are a sinner and have accepted His Son, Jesus, as your Savior, then all your sins are forgiven—past, present, and future—and you have eternal life (see John 3:14-18). What John was saying was that when we sin, we must confess the sin to God so we can be back in fellowship with Him.

2. Ask your support partner or a close friend to show you any "blind spots" you may have concerning your attitude toward your spouse. Michelle and I rarely counsel couples together. Our particular calling seems to be with those whose spouses are unwilling to work on the marriage. Because of that, Michelle sees women alone, and I meet with men alone. More often than not, the unwilling spouse comes around about halfway through our classes or counseling sessions. When he or she does, we are usually surprised to see that the spouse who was refusing to come to the first portion of the class or counseling session, wasn't really a monster after all. In many cases, these couples reconcile. Just as we did when our own marriage was in crisis, a spouse who has been hurt usually paints an untrue picture of his or her mate because all that spouse focuses on on is the negative behavior.

Jesus spoke of the importance of first dealing with your own negative behavior before judging someone else's: "Why do you look at the speck of sawdust in your brother's eye and pay no attention to the plank in your own eye? . . . You hypocrite, first take the plank out of your own eye, and then you will see clearly to remove the speck from your brother's eye" (Matthew 7:3-5). If you are focusing on the "speck" in your spouse's eye, it will be difficult to hear what God wants to say to you.

In his book *Hope for the Separated*, Dr. Gary Chapman writes: "I have often given individuals (in my counseling sessions) a sheet of paper and asked them to list the faults of their spouses. They will write profusely for ten or fifteen minutes. Some have even asked for more paper. The lists are magnificent and detailed. When I ask them to make a list of their own faults, they immediately list their one big fault. That is followed with a long period of silence as they try to think of number two. Some never find it, and seldom has anyone come back with more than four personal faults."[8]

3. Open God's Word and expect to hear from Him. I (Joe) like to refer to the Bible as the "Mind of God." When I open it, I expect to hear from Him. Sometimes, He speaks to me through a particular scripture, other times through a story or example. There were times during our separation when I was just learning to study the Bible and I didn't know where certain passages were located, but I knew if I just kept reading, God would give me something. I always tell my Thursday-night guys, "If you want to know the will of God, then open up the Mind of God—the Bible—or you'll never hear Him."

I (Michelle) went to a women's retreat right after Joe and I separated the second time. The speaker said, "Spending 15 minutes a day in the Bible will change your life in ways you never dreamed possible." I was raised with the idea that you read Scripture once a week at church or memorized portions of it during a midweek class for a grade. It had never occurred to me to read the Bible daily, just for the purpose of getting in touch with God. The idea that it didn't have to involve hours of study to make a difference gave me hope. I think people often don't read the Bible because they think they have to be in a Bible study or at church in order to open it. But that's not true. Religion says you pick up the "Mind of God" only when you are in a structured setting. Religion also says you must spend hours a day reading the Bible in order to grow close to God. Not that a structured study or hours in the Word isn't good for you, but 15 minutes a day is enough to change your life, and it's certainly better than not reading God's Word at all.

4. Forgive your spouse and ask your spouse to forgive you. When a marriage is in crisis forgiveness is very difficult, yet it is the most important step to take when God seems silent. Read what the psalmist writes in Psalm 86:5-7: "You are forgiving and good, O Lord, abounding in love to all who call to you. Hear my prayer, O LORD; listen to my cry for mercy. In the day of my trouble I will call to you, for you will answer me."

God is a forgiving God and because we are forgiven, we must forgive others as well. You may be saying to yourself right now, *But I'm not the one who needs to be forgiven! I haven't done anything wrong!* We understand. Both of us felt that way more than once when our marriage was in crisis, and many people we talk with have felt the same.

But reflect on the quote from Gary Chapman about making a list of your spouse's faults. It's important to take responsibility for your *own* faults. On the other hand, don't overly focus on dredging up a laundry list of things you *think* you have done that offended your spouse. That could backfire and cause more offenses. People have told us they were upset when their spouses made a list of supposed offenses and then demanded to be forgiven for them. One man said, "My wife started reading off this long list of things I never even remembered her doing! I certainly wasn't offended by them, so how was I supposed to forgive her? I felt manipulated and forced into saying, 'Yes, I forgive you' just to have the conversation end."

During our separation, Michelle met with our pastor to get advice because she felt frustrated that we kept dragging things up from the past. The pastor suggested that she say this sentence to me: "Would you please forgive me for not being the wife you have needed me to be?" When she asked me to forgive her using those words, it created a different atmosphere immediately, and I asked her to forgive me as well. Even though we didn't reconcile until several months later, that sentence stimulated a breakthrough in our communication. We refer to that sentence the pastor gave her as the "Forgiveness Sentence" and it works well in any relationship. Ken and Jane are perfect examples.

When Jane called our ministry, she had given up hope that her marriage with Ken could be saved. Her relationship with him was so bad that nothing seemed capable of stopping the downward spiral. Michelle suggested Jane say the "Forgiveness Sentence" to Ken. A few days later, Jane and Ken showed up at a reconciliation seminar at our church and made a commitment to work on their marriage. Jane said the sentence started them on the road to reconciliation. Ken said later, "When she worded her request to forgive her like that, it seemed to stop everything from escalating. We put down our weapons, and I saw hope."

That was in 1996. Today Ken and Jane are founders of a large nonprofit ministry in Turlock, California, called Prodigal Sons and Daughters,[9] which offers help to troubled teens and their parents.

Forgiveness is the first step to reconciliation. Without forgiveness, a couple who get back together simply pulls the rug over their issues. Eventually their marriage will be in crisis again. That's what Joe and I did for years. But when we started taking responsibility to "let go" of offenses—even if we never saw eye to eye on the offenses—our marriage started turning around. One mistake we see a lot of couples make is thinking they can't forgive their spouses unless their spouses ask. The problem with that thinking is that so often—especially in marriage—a spouse never asks. One reason for this is that many people see offenses differently. For instance, suppose you thought your spouse snapped and was rude to you in front of a friend or relative. Later, you confront your spouse and he or she says something like, "What are you talking about! I was not rude . . . *you* were!" Now, what are you going to do? Your spouse could say "I'm sorry" and not mean it. Or you could say "I'm sorry" and not mean it. To say "I'm sorry" just so someone can forgive you is pointless because it's not real.

If you want to remain real and avoid a false apology, you have three options: First, you could walk away angry and stay angry until your spouse sees things your way. Second, you could harbor bitterness because your spouse never sees it your way. Or third, after speaking the truth (in love) you could choose to forgive your spouse and give the offense over to God (see Jesus' response to insults and hatred in Luke 23:34). The key when someone is unrepentant or ignorant is not pretending (we discuss this in more detail in chapters 6 and 7), but instead giving the offense over to God and not harboring unforgiveness.

The act of forgiveness involves an action of only one person, while reconciliation requires a response from both parties. If we had to wait for others to repent before we forgave them, often we would have to wait forever!

The following action step provides an easy means of helping remove the barrier of unforgiveness in order to reconcile with your spouse.

5. Spend time alone with the Lord and rest in His silence. One of the things that helps both of us draw closer to God and feel His presence when we are confused is to get away and spend time alone with Him. This has become a tool that we share with everyone because we know how well it works.

Jesus spent hours alone praying to His Father, and He modeled the importance of going to God when we need to know His will. If you are feeling confused and need to hear from God, draw close to Him and allow Him to meet you in the midst of your circumstances. "Come near to God and he will come near to you" (James 4:8).

Joe and I like to spend time alone with God differently. Joe can be alone with God out in the yard or even washing his car, but I can't seem to get away from daily pressures unless I'm away from the house. If you are like me, you may want to do what I did when I wanted some quality time alone with God. After reading a booklet on how to spend a day with God, I used it as a model to create my own overnight getaway with the Lord.

Preparation: If going away overnight doesn't put too much stress or financial strain on you, it is a great way to get alone with God. Even if you aren't able to be gone overnight, try to choose a quiet setting away from home, such as the ocean, a favorite fishing spot, or anywhere that displays the beauty of nature. Bring your Bible, a notebook, a Bible concordance, and a devotional—I like *My Utmost for His Highest.*

Morning: Get an early start and use the first portion of the day to thank God for everything that comes to mind. Focus on the beauty of your surroundings. Take your time and ask God to bring to mind everything you are grateful for. Use your concordance to look up words such as *love, thanksgiving,* and *grace.* Find passages in the Bible to help you stay focused.

Afternoon: Ask God to bring to mind anyone (other than your spouse, since you are already working on that relationship) whom you need to forgive and/or reconcile with. Write down their names and pray for them. If you list someone who has abused you, we are not suggesting you should go back to your abuser to reconcile (we will discuss abusive relationships more in depth in chapter 8). However, keep in mind that forgiveness is still the first step in reconciling any relationship.

If God reminds you of someone who has something against you, pray for His will in the situation. This is an important part of your day with God because He warns us about coming to the altar when we know that someone has something against us: "Therefore if you are presenting your offering at the altar, and there remember that your brother has something against you, leave your offering there before the altar and go; first be reconciled to your brother, and then come and present your offering" (Matthew 5:23-24, NASB).

Regarding your marriage, pray that God will enable you to see your spouse through His eyes to better understand how to respond to his or her needs when you return home. Your response needs to be focused on pleasing God as the priority.

Evening: The last portion of the day is used to determine how you are using the gifts and talents God has given you, based on Romans 12:6-8. For example, if you have the gift of teaching, have you considered enrolling in a course to study the Bible for the purpose of teaching others? Could your church use help in any of the areas in which God has naturally gifted you? If you are unsure what your spiritual gifts are after reading the verses in Romans, consider taking a "spiritual gifts test" when you return home.[10]

6. Stay focused on God—even if you don't feel like it. After Michelle and I had been back together for a couple of years, we drove across the country for a vacation. On the way back home, we went through Utah on a road referred to as "The Loneliest Highway in America." We stopped at a gas station and found the gas too overpriced for my taste, so I decided to drive on and find another station down the road. I should have realized the next station on that lonely highway would have prices double those charged at the first. Needless to say, as my gas gauge edged near empty, I was willing to pay anything.

That experience led me to create the "Spiritual Fuel Tank Indicator"—a gauge to monitor our "spiritual tanks." When we need filling, God is right there to fill us up. Yet we tend to travel down the highway of life going our own way until our spiritual tanks are on empty. Only then are we willing to get filled up with God again.

This tool doesn't take anyone else's participation to work. It helps Michelle and I keep our focus where it needs to be, rather than where it used to be. Instead of getting all worked up when things aren't going the way we think they should, we have learned to focus on the Spirit of God and be filled up with Him.

The next time you start to feel uneasy about anything, remind yourself that you have two choices: You can avoid prayer, which will move you in the direction of your own will, or you can shift your focus to prayer and eventually move the spiritual indicator to God. Shifting your focus at the *first* sign of uneasiness will keep you full of Him

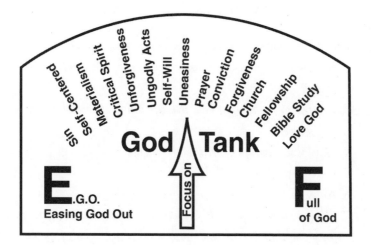

GOD IS ALWAYS THERE

Your enemy Satan wants you to feel hopeless. One way he does this is by deceiving you into believing God has abandoned you. Once you believe the lie that God doesn't care about your problems, you will no longer go to Him in prayer, and you will become a sitting duck for Satan's ploys. The truth is, if you have prayed to receive Christ as your Savior, you are God's child and He will never abandon you: "Never will I leave you; never will I forsake you" (Hebrews 13:5).

One reason you may be waiting for your marriage to be completely healed is that God may be working on your spouse's heart. But another reason you might be suffering in a crisis marriage is because

God is allowing your own heart to break so He can enter in. In the next chapter we will discuss how God can even use wrong motives of the heart to achieve His perfect will.

GROUP OR SUPPORT-PARTNER
DISCUSSION QUESTIONS

1. *Are you seeking God's help in your present situation? If so, how?*
2. *Based on the examples in this chapter, how does God answer prayer?*
3. *Have you ever felt that God was unwilling or unable to answer your prayers?*
4. *Have you ever experienced God's "silence"?*
5. *Look up and discuss Philippians 4:6-7.*
6. *Name at least one thing you are thankful for.*
7. *Share a prayer request. If you have never prayed as a couple and are going through the book with your spouse, try praying for each other. If your spouse is not willing or able to pray, pray with your support partner or small group if you feel comfortable doing that.*

Identify Secret Motives

Search me, O God, and know my heart; test me and
know my anxious thoughts.

—PSALM 139:23

O ver the years, we've realized the issue of motives runs rampant in counseling sessions and reconciliation classes. We
know from our own past, as well as our experience with others, that
much of what is said in the beginning of a marriage crisis is based on
hidden agendas and motives of one or both spouses. Author and
licensed counselor Dr. Robert Ross wrote to us recently in agreement:
"I often see couples who come to counseling even though one of them
has already made a secret decision to divorce. He/she will go through
the motions so they can say, 'Well, we tried everything and nothing
worked.' "[1]

We know that hundreds of couples each year attend seminars and
weekend retreats hoping to rekindle the romance in their marriages,
and many do so because their marriages are in severe crisis. Jill, for
example, convinced her husband, Ben, to attend a Marriage Alive[2]
seminar in 2003 as a last-ditch effort to save their marriage. It worked,
and they are still together today. There are countless testimonies from
couples who say their broken marriages were healed because they
sought counseling as a couple or attended a weekend marriage event.

However, it is a misconception to think that your motives for attending counseling or marriage seminars together are automatically the same. Half the time, we don't even know our own motives, much less someone else's. "The heart is deceitful above all things and beyond cure. Who can understand it?" (Jeremiah 17:9). But God can even use wrong motives to accomplish His will, just as He did in Mark and Debbie's marriage.

Mark and Debbie attended a reconciliation class that we taught at our church several years ago, but their motives weren't the same. "I was attending so that when our marriage ended in divorce, our children couldn't say that their dad was the only one who tried to save it," Debbie now says, recalling the first time she walked into class. "Our arguments had gotten so volatile that at one point, the police were involved. The first several weeks of the class, I was living a lie. I attended, did the homework, and participated in the discussions, even though I didn't believe God could change my life or heal our marriage. I didn't trust God, and I definitely didn't trust Christians. I'd had a bad experience in church during my younger years and all I'd known was hypocrisy. So when our class leaders told us to focus on God and create a support system with other Christians, I honestly expected everyone—including God—to leave me once I wasn't living up to people's expectations."

As the weeks passed, it became more difficult for Debbie to keep up her false pretenses, and she began to share her struggles openly. "I couldn't keep pretending. Finally, I just decided to tell the women in my group how I really felt. Instead of feeling judged and condemned, the women in my discussion group surprised me by showing compassion and even sharing some of their own struggles. Little by little, my heart began to soften toward God and others, and I started practicing what I was learning in class."

That was back in 1994. God did a miracle in Mark and Debbie's marriage despite her secret motives in the beginning. Today, they serve as national ministry coleaders with us, and they are committed to God and to each other.

Mark's compassion is evident when he speaks to people about keeping their focus on God regardless of what their spouses do: "If you are trying your best but aren't seeing progress in your marriage, don't give up! Pray for your spouse daily. Keep your focus on God— not your spouse—and trust Him with the outcome of your marriage. 'Trust in the LORD with all your heart and lean not on your own understanding; in all your ways acknowledge him, and he will make your paths straight'" (Proverbs 3:5-6).

GOD WILL REVEAL WRONG MOTIVES IN HIS TIME

You might be asking yourself how you can know if your spouse's motives are pure. You might even be admitting that *you* are the one whose motives are not completely honest. It doesn't matter which end of the spectrum you are on; God knows your spouse's heart and He knows yours as well. God will reveal wrong motives in His time. Take a few moments to privately answer the following questions:

- Can you think of at least five reasons why you want to remain married to your spouse?
- What reasons come to your mind as to why you might want to end your marriage?
- Have you ever attended couples-focused counseling or a marriage seminar but didn't really want to? Did you tell your spouse how you honestly felt?
- Do you think your spouse has ever attended counseling or a marriage-related event simply to appease you, rather than to use what he or she learned to improve the marriage?

- Do emotional walls come between you and your spouse when certain hot-button issues are brought up? Can you recall those issues easily?
- How long has it been since you have told your spouse what you really think about important issues in your marriage?
- How long has it been since your spouse has truthfully shared his or her opinions or thoughts with you?
- If your spouse came to you today and confessed he or she was living a lie in your marriage, would you be able to listen to everything your spouse said, without shutting down emotionally or becoming aggressive?
- If you are not being real in your marriage, would you be willing right now to be real with God by confessing your fears and frustrations to Him—regardless of how you think your spouse would react?

While these questions are here for you to answer privately, remember that God sees into your heart. The Lord's words to His servant Samuel in the Old Testament are still a reminder for us today: "Man looks at the outward appearance, but the LORD looks at the heart" (1 Samuel 16:7).

Pastor and professor Dr. Warren Wiersbe writes in *Be Real*, "If we live to please men, we will always be in trouble because no two men will agree and we will find ourselves caught in the middle. Walking in the light—living to please God—simplifies our goals, unifies our lives, and gives us a sense of peace and poise."[3]

BEING REAL MAY CAUSE OTHERS TO SUFFER

One couple we ministered to several years ago reconciled after being separated nearly a year. They even began serving in ministry at their church helping other couples in crisis. Three years later we got a call from the wife saying that shortly after they reconciled, her husband began having another affair and was living a double life—even while serving in ministry. When he finally decided to be real, it wasn't for the purpose of repenting; it was because he couldn't continue living a double life any longer. Having the truth exposed meant the end of their marriage and pain for many in their church and family, but the woman told us, "As much as it hurt to find out he was living a lie all that time, I'd rather suffer knowing the truth than have a false peace believing a lie."

Curt and Debra are another couple who thought their reconciliation was real and yet continued to struggle. Debra thought she and Curt had a good marriage with no secrets between them. That is, until Curt went on an extended trip to help his dying mother. "While Curt was gone, I found a credit card I didn't even know we had. When I questioned Curt about it, he admitted that he had been hiding a gambling problem for quite some time."

"I tried to tell Debra several times," Curt said when they gave their testimony several years later. "I wanted to get help, but I was afraid Debra would leave me if she found out how much money we owed on that card."

He was wrong; Debra didn't leave. They both worked hard and paid off the debt and Curt promised never to gamble again. All was well—until it happened again two years later. This time Curt didn't get caught. God convicted him, and he willingly confessed to Debra, their church, and family. However, even though Curt told the truth on his own this time, it was not without consequences. Debra recalls, "When he told me he had started gambling again, it was so much worse the second time around. The first time it happened I took some of the blame because he said he was afraid to tell me. But he couldn't say that this time! I had been there for him, and he let me down. I made him move out because I thought I could never trust him to tell me the truth again."

Curt moved out and sought help through a ministry for people with gambling addictions. While he and Debra were separated, they worked on their individual issues. Debra attended women's Bible studies while Curt faithfully worked through the addiction program and reconciled with all the people he had deceived in previous years.

Debra took the risk to reconcile with him nearly two years later. "I realized I had to entrust Curt to God and that if I found out he was dishonest again, I'd just have to cross that bridge when I came to it. What gave me the most comfort was that he had decided to bring his addiction out in the open the second time because he wanted to do what was right, no matter what my response was."

"I knew it was going to cause pain for everyone when I decided to tell the truth, but I also knew I couldn't get the help I needed unless I did," Curt admitted to us just before they reconciled.

~⊙~

Sometimes, you might suffer because your spouse has risked being real with you. That's what happened one night between Joe and me. At one point during our separation I was feeling lonely and insecure and decided to go to Joe's apartment. Our son was there for the weekend, and when I showed up uninvited with an overnight bag, Joe was surprised—and at first, pleased. His expression changed, however, when he found out why I was there: "Joe, all I want to do is spend the night—no strings attached—and just have you hold me in your arms because I'm feeling lonely."

A frown came across Joe's face and his response took me by surprise. He had been asking me to reconcile for so long that I expected him to gladly welcome me for the night. In the past, we had spent several nights together during our separation. *After all, we are still married,* I would tell myself, even though I didn't want him to move back home yet. But things were about to change.

"Michelle, you can't just come over and spend the night when you want to. I don't want bits and pieces of you anymore. It's too hard on me."

"Fine," I said, trying to appear confident while fighting back tears. "Then I won't ever spend the night with you again!" Although I held my head high as I turned and walked away, inside I felt scared, lonely, and worst of all, rejected. As I drove away, I couldn't hold the tears back any longer. Sobbing, I cried aloud, partly in prayer and partly out of frustration, "God, all I wanted to do was spend the night with Joe and have him hold me in his arms so I wouldn't feel so lonely. I can't believe he would turn me away. I've never known this kind of rejection before. I have no one to turn to."

At that moment Jesus' presence was so real that I turned to look at the empty seat beside me. It was as if He were sitting there speaking directly into my heart: "Michelle, every time you have been lonely or scared, I've been there with outstretched arms waiting for you to run to Me. Instead, you have always run right past Me and into the arms of a man. When will you let Me be the One to hold you when you are lonely and scared?" By this time, I was home and my tears were no longer falling because of my feelings of rejection. They were falling from my repentant heart. Since my teen years, my significance and self-worth had come only from men, and I'd missed the truth that Jesus' arms were the only ones that would never let me go.

Joe was real with me that night and his words hurt, but his rejection helped me realize my need to depend on Jesus in a new way.

Once I was completely real with the Lord, He was able to fill the loneliness in my heart once and for all. My new dependence on God came as a result of Joe's honest confrontation.

GOD CAN EVEN USE OUR WRONG MOTIVES

Several weeks after the incident at Joe's apartment, one of the pastors from our church called to ask if I would be willing to meet with Joe for six weeks of counseling.

"Has Joe agreed?" I asked, secretly hoping that he hadn't.

"Yes, Joe was very agreeable," the pastor answered.

"Oh, sure, I'm willing to meet too," I said. I was glad the pastor couldn't see the look of frustration on my face. Even though I was learning to depend on God for my significance, Joe and I still had a lot of unresolved issues in our marriage.

I was not looking forward to meeting with Joe on a weekly basis and had no desire to move back in together. I'd grown accustomed to being separated. Sure, there were times I missed being a wife and a homemaker, but the fear of fighting and arguing all the time stopped me from taking the risk to reconcile. I expected to be separated for a long time—maybe the rest of my life—so six weeks of couples counseling seemed a waste of time. Secretly, I hoped that Joe wouldn't show up for the first appointment, but that didn't happen. When I arrived at the church the first week, Joe's truck was in the parking lot. Early, no less!

Fine, I thought. *He wants us to meet as a couple for six weeks? Well, he's going to hear everything he ever did that caused our marriage to fail. Maybe he'll even walk out like he has in the past, and then the pastor will see why communicating with Joe is impossible.*

～☙～

When the pastor called to ask me to meet with him and Michelle, I was encouraged because I wanted Michelle to be confronted with her unwillingness to reconcile. I had stopped drinking and was doing everything possible to get her to agree that it was not in God's will for us to be separated. But it seemed the harder I tried to convince Michelle, the more she pulled away. That's why I was looking forward to our counseling sessions as a couple. I was sure the pastor would convince her to let me move back home. At our first appointment, Pastor Phil began with questions like these:

- "What do you think needs to change in order for the two of you to reconcile?"
- "What are some positive changes you have seen in one another?"
- "Are there any areas in your lives that you are not taking responsibility for?"

He was trying to take notes, but we were interrupting each other and arguing so much that at one point he put his pen down, raised his hands to heaven as if he were praying, and begged us to stop arguing.

I'm certain that the pastor received some counsel himself in order to prepare for our next meeting, because the following week, he had some ground rules in place. When we entered his office, his voice was more authoritative. He told us there would be no interrupting, and he warned that if we argued, he would get up and wait in the hall until we were through bickering, and had quieted down.

You'd think we would have been too embarrassed to interrupt and argue after his admonition. Not so. Every time the pastor asked us a question over which we had unresolved issues, the ground rules went right out the door. When one of us interrupted the other, the pastor would raise his arms high and say, "Now, now . . . there you go interrupting again! Joe, let her finish" or "Michelle, let him finish." It was hard not to get defensive when I felt attacked by Michelle. It was even harder to sit there and not walk out, but I suspected that was what Michelle wanted, and I didn't want to give her the satisfaction.

~_๑~

When Joe and I were in those counseling sessions, it was as if a flood-gate opened. I was completely honest and left no stone unturned. Over the years, I had learned to suppress my opinions and feelings as a way of avoiding conflict and keeping Joe from leaving and going to a bar. Secretly hoping he would walk out during the counseling sessions, I no longer feared his reactions and had nothing to lose except the marriage, which I didn't want anyway.

Joe could take only so much of my "honesty" before blowing up, and we'd get into a heated argument that would send the pastor into the hallway for a while. Surprisingly though, Joe never walked out. We met for six weeks and the pastor never hurried us. Sometimes, we were there for as long as two hours. I didn't count all the times the pastor went into the hall, and I remember very little about what he said. In fact, I now realized that he mostly refereed and provided us a place to argue with guidelines. It was difficult for either one of us to leave or not show up because that would have caused the other person to appear more committed to the marriage and thus become the "winner." Nevertheless, in spite of our stubborn self-centered motives, God never gave up on us and the counseling sessions played a major role in our reconciliation a couple of months later.

~_๑~

When Michelle started unleashing her feelings in our counseling sessions, I was surprised. I had never seen her be so bold about what she really thought and felt. She took a hard stand with me regarding the way I had behaved in our marriage—especially in the area of my drinking and leaving in the middle of conflict. I didn't like what I heard, but at least I finally knew what she was thinking. Her words reflected and aligned with the ways she had behaved all those years. Michelle admitted that at times she had been hurt or frustrated, but instead of being honest she pretended things were okay because she wanted a nice Christmas or a fun vacation, or simply wanted to avoid conflict so that I wouldn't leave. She also said that she had lost respect and love for me over the years because of my ungodly behavior when things got stressful.

Of course, I told Michelle some things too, but she had heard me say them many times before. When the six weeks of counseling were over, I was disappointed that we hadn't reconciled. Instead, our situation looked even more hopeless. Not long afterward, however, something happened that changed my focus from saving our marriage to trusting God—regardless of whether or not we ever got back together.

Two weeks after our counseling sessions ended, Michelle decided to take a trip to Alaska (where she lived before we got together) to visit some friends she had stayed in contact with over the past nine years. I offered to drive her to the airport and tried to act as if I didn't care that she was going. But in the back of my mind, I was worried that she would want to live in Alaska again, and then we'd never reconcile.

One night about a week after she left, I prayed to God and asked Him to help me trust her. I felt God saying to me, "You can't trust Michelle—or anyone else for that matter. You can trust only *Me,* and you can entrust Michelle *to* Me."

During the weeks she was gone, I spent time before the Lord, giving Michelle and our marriage to Him for the first time. I began to understand that she had been my "little god." Instead of trusting in

God, I had been trusting in myself to save our marriage. I was focused on keeping Michelle as my wife because I didn't think I could ever be happy otherwise. I finally recognized this behavior as idolatrous.

In the first two commandments in Exodus 20:3-4, God said, "You shall have no other gods before me" and "You shall not make for yourself an idol . . . for I am a jealous God" (NASB). Once I repented I felt like a new man. Finally, I could honestly believe that life with or without Michelle would not determine my happiness. God was my focus and the only One I would worship. Michelle was free to live her life as she chose, and I was finally free.

REAL MOTIVES, REAL LOVE

When Joe picked me up from the airport after I returned from Alaska, he looked like a different man. He was more appealing, better looking, and more confident. "What's different?" I asked, trying to decide if he had gotten a haircut or new clothes.

"Nothing. Why do you ask?" he answered.

"No reason. You just look different." I kept staring at him when he wasn't looking.

The next day I told my friend Karin that Joe looked handsome when he picked me up at the airport.

"Are you feeling attracted to him? Is there any chance of the two of you reconciling?" she asked smiling.

"No," I lied. "Are you kidding? Don't even think about us getting back together."

A couple of weeks later God revealed the six hot-button issues in our marriage to me as I was walking and praying on the beach. Because Joe's focus had shifted from me to God, he was more concerned about saying what was right, rather than what he thought he should say to convince me to reconcile with him. His total dependence on God made him feel secure in himself for the first time, and his confidence made him very attractive to me.

In *My Utmost for His Highest,* Oswald Chambers says, "No one enters into the experience of entire sanctification without going through a 'white funeral'—the burial of the old life. . . . Nothing can upset such a life, it is one with God for one purpose, to be a witness to Him. . . . Is there a place to which the memory goes back with a chastened and extraordinarily grateful remembrance—'Yes, it was then, at that 'white funeral,' that I made an agreement with God.' "[4]

I had my "white funeral" when Joe refused to let me stay the night with him, and Joe had his when he thought I was going to move back to Alaska. We both recall these events as major turning points in our reconciliation because God became our main focus rather than each other. We were finally on our way to kicking the habit of needing to be "high" on anything or anyone but Jesus.

TAKE THE RISK TO BE REAL

It's not easy to listen to criticism or hear your spouse tell you things he or she would like you to change. But if you are going to have true intimacy and reconciliation, you will have to take the risk to be real and help your spouse do the same. The following exercise can be used with your spouse or any person with whom you have a broken relationship or an emotional wall. It is especially helpful with teens.

First, ask your support system to pray for you. You won't want to do this exercise without a lot of prayer support. The potential for anger outbursts and hurt feelings is high when you give people permission to tell you something they have been holding back because they feared your response. So ask your support team to pray that God would give you the wisdom, courage, and discernment to know what to say.

Second, choose an appropriate time. Timing is everything when engaging in this exercise. Be sensitive to the surroundings and your spouse's mood. For instance, tired and hungry people who are in the middle of a task or under stress will not want to discuss a serious topic. *Well, then, forget that,* you may be thinking, *because the person I want to do this exercise with will never have time to discuss a serious topic I initiate.* Hold on. Remember that the first step is prayer. God will give you wisdom without reproach if you ask. "But if any of you lacks wisdom, let him ask of God, who gives to all generously and without reproach, and it will be given to him" (James 1:5, NASB).

Third, ask the following questions and pray silently: "Have you ever avoided telling me how you really feel or think? Is there anything you want to tell me now?" Silently pray and wait. Your spouse may test the waters first by saying a few things to see if you'll get angry. For instance, if you are doing this exercise with a teen, he or she may grunt something like, "Yeah, right, and then you'll go into one of your fits of rage and I'll be grounded for the next year." A disgruntled spouse may say, "Why should I answer? You never listen anyway." Some people have even said that their spouses looked at them with expressions of, "Do you think I'm crazy? I'm not going there!" It may take several attempts over a period of time to let your spouse know that you aren't going to flip out or shut down if you hear something you don't like. This is a risk, to be sure, but it's important to remember that whatever your spouse or loved one is keeping from you is in his or her heart anyway. Telling you what he or she is feeling simply puts it out into the light where you can work on it together. Your enemy the Devil wants to keep it in the dark, but God wants to bring it into the light.

Last, listen and ask clarifying questions. When Jesus spoke to people, He asked intentional questions and was not reactive. He gave them a safe place to be real. Learn to do the same with those you love. Even if you hear something that you don't agree with or don't like, this is not the time or place to get defensive. If you do, you will simply put the wall back up. By listening, silently praying, and asking clarifying questions in order to keep the person engaged, you are setting an example as well as helping to bring truth into the light. Consider asking these questions:

- How am I contributing to the breakdown in our communication?
- What can I do to make our home a happier place to be?
- Do I ever put pressure on you to be someone you aren't?
- What do you wish I would stop doing?

Obviously, you will have to guard against the urge to tell your loved one all the things you wish he or she would change. But this exercise isn't supposed to be used for that purpose. It is designed to provide a safe place for someone else to be real with you. The exercises in chapters 7 and 8 will deal with the importance of bringing *your* issues and concerns into the light and they will help you be real with others—even when you are afraid.

WHAT'S YOUR SUBTEXT?

Several years ago, an actor told us she was once in a play in which the director would often walk by and shout "*Subtext!*" as actors rehearsed their lines. The director would do that only if he thought the inflection in their voices or body language wasn't lining up with the plot—or subtext—of the scene. He knew the audience would be confused if their lines were delivered in a way that contradicted the subtext of the play.

While we are not actors on a stage rehearsing for a play, it would probably do us well at times to imagine God—the great Director of our lives—calling out to us, "*Subtext!*" and our saying back to Him, "Your will and not mine, Lord."

As you learn to place your trust completely in God's hands and let Him guide the direction of your life, it is our prayer that you will have your own "white funeral." Once you do, you will be able to access the supernatural power of the Holy Spirit living within you and live life to the fullest regardless of what your spouse chooses to do. God has given you a unique personality that was meant to be used in conjunction with His Holy Spirit. Are you enjoying what God has given you? Or, have you been so preoccupied with your crisis marriage that you don't even know who you are anymore?

In the next chapter, we will talk about why some couples divorce because their spouses have changed . . . or could it be they are suffering from an empty love tank?

GROUP OR SUPPORT-PARTNER DISCUSSION QUESTIONS

1. *Discuss the five reasons you want to stay married.*
2. *Have you ever put your spouse in the place that God should have in your life?*
3. *Discuss what a "white funeral" would look like for you.*
4. *Have you discussed any of these tools or exercises with your spouse?*
5. *Look up and discuss the Ten Commandments from Exodus 20.*
6. *Share something that you are thankful for in your life.*
7. *Share a prayer request. (If you are able and willing, continue praying with your spouse, support partner, or small group each week. If you have never kept a journal to write down prayer requests and answers to prayer, consider starting one now.)*

Spouses May Change After Marriage

And we, who with unveiled faces all reflect the Lord's glory, are being transformed into his likeness with ever-increasing glory, which comes from the Lord, who is the Spirit.

—2 CORINTHIANS 3:18

*S*everal months before Joe and I reconciled, I went to his apartment to drop off our son and noticed he had done some redecorating. "Well, this is unusual décor," I said, scrutinizing the changes. His coffee table had been traded in for a treasure chest, and Mickey Mouse pictures replaced the wall hangings he had taken from our house when we first separated. There were frog planters on the end tables, stuffed animal pillows on his couch, and a stand-up carousal in the corner of the living room. "This looks more like a toy store instead of a grown man's apartment" I said, rolling my eyes.

"I've decorated my apartment like this so that Mick can have fun when he comes over," Joe said, sounding irritated. "You know, Michelle, you've changed. You're so serious lately. Maybe you just need to lighten up and have some fun in your life once in a while."

"*I've* changed?" I decided to leave before a battle could start, but not before having the last word. In a most mature voice, I replied,

"Well, maybe I should dress like Snow White and we could all just live happily ever after." Feeling very smug, I walked out the door. Seeing Joe's bright yellow truck in the driveway—newly painted with flames—I muttered, "We could never live together again. We've definitely grown apart, and Joe just isn't even the same person anymore."

～❧～

When Michelle and I were first married, there was a nice balance of work and fun in our life. Sure, we had our problems, but even so, we accomplished a lot as a couple. We opened our own business the first year we were married, and had fun doing it. I am more spontaneous and less structured than Michelle but when we first met, I didn't notice our differences that much. When I called and asked her to go out on a date, she never said, "Sure, but only after the laundry is done." There were lots of times that she would drop everything just to drive to the beach overnight—even after Mick was born. Later on, though, when things got more stressful in our marriage, I'd want to be spontaneous and go somewhere and Michelle would respond as if I was being irresponsible. She'd say something such as, "I thought you said you were going to work in the yard today" or "Joe, can't you see that there are a million things to do around here? Am I just supposed to drop everything and play all the time?" By the time our last separation occurred, we didn't seem to have anything in common anymore. Michelle accused me of changing, but I thought she was the one who had changed.

Natural Strengths Can Become Weaknesses

It's not unusual for couples to blame their marital problems on one or both of them changing after they married. But that's a misconception.

The truth is, we all have strengths and weaknesses in our natural personalities that never change. However, at times, under stressful circumstances, people may *seem* like they've changed. Mels Carbonell, author and creator of the *Uniquely You in Christ* personality and spiritual-gifts test, explains it this way: "The Bible confirms that you were *wonderfully* made (Psalm 139:14). God's plan and purpose was to create a person *uniquely You*. He gifted you to glorify Him with specific influences—naturally and supernaturally. As a Christian, you have a God-given personality and spiritual gifts that motivate you. Every personality has strengths and weaknesses. . . . Always remember that under pressure you lean toward your strengths."[1] Corbonell then warns that leaning on his or her strengths to the extreme can cause a person to act out in their weaknesses: "The overuse of a strength becomes an abuse, and the best thing about you becomes the worst. The characteristic that people once liked most about you can become what they later despise."[2]

Since pressure can cause people to behave differently, it is easy to understand why a person might think his or her spouse has changed after marriage. After all, is there any other relationship on earth more challenging than a marriage? The apostle Paul even warned those he taught to consider staying single: "But those who marry will face many troubles in this life" (1 Corinthians 7:28).

Marriage is difficult for many reasons. For one, we have to learn to live with—or *tolerate*—our many differences. Almost all relationship experts agree with Dr. Carbonell's descriptions of personality strengths and weaknesses, and how challenging it is to live in harmony with those we love.

Before two people marry, it seems like nothing can keep them apart, but once the honeymoon is over, everything seems to keep them apart. We get frustrated with our spouses because after marriage they "change" into someone we don't like, or we marry someone and hope we can change him or her—but our spouse stays the same. Our pastor once said, "Married couples are like flies on a screen door: Those on the inside want out, and those on the outside want in!"

~❦~

Even after Joe and I reconciled, we kept trying to change each other rather than accept each other's differences. I tried to make him more goal oriented, and he tried to get me to be more spontaneous. I thought there was something wrong with Joe because "fun" to him was waking up in the morning and facing a day that had no particular order or time factor to deal with, and he thought something was wrong with me because I considered a "fun day" to be one with a long to-do list and a crunching deadline looming overhead. Then, several months after we were back together, we saw a video series at our church titled "Your Personality Tree" by Fred and Florence Littauer.[3] What we learned that weekend revolutionized our marriage. We finally understood that our personality temperaments were God-given and that there was nothing wrong with either one of us—we were just wired differently.

The Four Basic Temperaments

The Greek philosopher Hippocrates was the first to describe the four basic temperaments to the world in 400 B.C. Over the past several years, well-known Christian authors and speakers, including the Littauers, have referred to these personality types using their own descriptions, tests, and titles. The best-known titles are the ones coined by Hippocrates: *Sanguine, Choleric, Melancholy,* and *Phlegmatic.* Over the years, we combined the teachings of others to create our own explanation and temperament test. While everyone has some characteristics of each temperament, one will usually be more evident. Take a few moments to take the test. Even if you have taken one before, this will help you when applying the tools in the rest of the chapter.

Temperament Test

After studying the four choices across, please circle the word or sentence that best or most often describes you. You will probably identify with all to a degree, but circle only the one that best applies. If you are not sure, ask someone who knows you well.

Strengths

Full of life	Risk taker	Analytical	Adapts to situations
Playful	Convincing	Finishes projects	Easy going
Social	Head strong	Self-sacrificing	Accepts rules
Funny	Commanding	Reliable	Friendly
Cheerful	Self-assured	Artistic	Even-tempered
Talkative	Goal oriented	Thoughtful	Tolerant
Lively	Leadership	Loyal	Good listener
Inspiring	Independent	Expects perfection	Agreeable
Optimistic	Outspoken	Organized	Accommodating

Subtotal your scores by adding the number of circles in each column, and go on to the next section.

Weaknesses

Undisciplined	Unsympathetic	Holds grudges	Lazy
Interrupts	Impatient	Never good enough	Indecisive
Too talkative	Inconsiderate	Easily offended	Peace at all cost
Naive	Overly confident	Negative	Unconcerned

Disorganized	Controlling	Depressed	Lack of confidence
Messy	Shrewd	Moody	Mumbles
Loud	Domineering	Avoids people	Too tired to work
Short attention span	Critical/judgmental	Manipulative	Too compromising
Inconsistent	Intolerant	Introvert	Indifferent

Subtotal the weaknesses, and then add together with strengths for the grand total.

Enter the strengths (from previous page). _____
Grand totals _____

Temperament Test Scores

The column with the highest total is your basic temperament. You might have close scores in other columns, but more than likely you will score high in one or two and lower (or not at all) in the other two columns. If you scored evenly across, you might want to ask your spouse, close friend, or family member to help you break the ties. While our goal is to be balanced in all the temperaments, most people aren't evenly balanced unless they have practiced a lot—or are Phlegmatics and have a difficult time making up their minds.

If you scored highest in the first column, you have a Sanguine personality. If you scored highest in the second, a Choleric personality. If you scored highest in the third, a Melancholy personality, and highest in the fourth, a Phlegmatic personality.

Temperament Descriptions
Sanguine—Jester
- Strengths: outgoing; energized by people and parties; spontaneous; forgives easily.

- Weaknesses: undisciplined; interrupts; doesn't listen; inconsistent.

Choleric—General

- Strengths: leader; goal oriented; convincing; self-assured.
- Weaknesses: unsympathetic; controlling; impatient; overly confident.

Melancholy—Officer

- Strengths: analytical; completes projects; detailed; reliable; expects perfection.
- Weaknesses: never good enough; negative; moody; easily offended.

Phlegmatic—Peacemaker

- Strengths: adaptable; easygoing; even-tempered; good listener; friendly.
- Weaknesses: lazy; indecisive; tired; indifferent.

Every Temperament Is Equally Important

All four temperaments are needed and one is not better than another. For example, imagine you were assigned to complete a group project in your church or workplace. The Choleric person would probably be in charge, and their mantra would be, "Hurry up, let's get this thing done!" The Sanguine person would want to make sure they were having fun. Their mantra would be, "Hey, let's order food and make sure there's music while we work." The Phlegmatic person would be waiting for orders from the leader, and their mantra would be, "I'm here to help! You can count on me—just tell me what you need and let's all get along!" The Melancholy person wouldn't be saying much because they would be focusing on all the important details the rest of the lot overlooked. Their mantra would be, "Don't forget to read the directions . . . and if you can't do this thing right, then don't do it at all!"

When people feel accepted and loved as they are, they will work in their strengths. As a result, completing group (or family) projects will create a sense of unity and much will be accomplished. On the other hand, when people feel judged and unaccepted, their strengths can become weaknesses. Consequently, group (and family) projects can become a source of conflict and little will get accomplished. The Choleric person will become bossy and demanding; the Sanguine person will leave—and when the project is complete, will throw a party and take all the credit; the Phlegmatic person will become physically ill because of the tension between everyone; and the Melancholy person will be so depressed that things aren't being done right, he or she won't come out of hiding for days.

COUPLES MARRY IN THEIR STRENGTHS, BUT SEPARATE IN THEIR WEAKNESSES

Opposites often attract because they appreciate the differences of the other person, and they are drawn to the strengths that they lack in their own temperaments. The Littauers agree this is common among couples: "When we focus on our partner's strengths, we are complementary to each other, but when we look at our differences, we have trouble. The frivolous Sanguine is (often) attracted to the serious Melancholy. The Choleric, who wants to lead, is (often) drawn to the Phlegmatic, who is willing to follow." [4]

Steve and Karen laugh about their differences now, but there was a time when they weren't so funny. "I am mostly Choleric and Steve is mostly Melancholy. I loved that Steve was a perfectionist, and I was drawn to his quiet nature and resolve to get things done right. A couple of years after we were married, I was upset with him for being gone so much that I started focusing on the weaknesses of his temperament. All the things I loved about his perfectionist personality began to drive me crazy—even how he licked the stamps to put on the envelopes after we paid bills! Instead of focusing on the fact that he always paid the bills on time, I grew irritated because it took him so long to stamp the envelopes. My choleric, goal-driven personality just wanted the job done. I would watch him eye the envelope, line the stamp up perfectly, and make sure every little thing was just right. So many times, I wanted to leap across the table, grab the stamp out of his hands, and just slap it on the envelope lopsided so I could make him as crazy as he was making me. We laugh about it now—although I must admit there are times I leave the room when he's going to stamp envelopes."

Eight Ways to Accept the Uniqueness of Your Spouse

1. Make a list of your spouse's strengths. Think back on the time when you and your spouse first met. Aside from the physical attraction you may have had, what qualities in his or her personality did you admire? What did you think about when you went home from your first date? Do you remember describing your future spouse to a friend after you realized you were falling in love? Again, aside from his or her physical appearance, what words did you use to describe the person you were falling in love with? These are the positive qualities of your spouse's natural temperament, and they are the strengths that first attracted you to him or her.

Using three-by-five cards, list as many positive qualities about your spouse as you. (Use the descriptions listed under your spouse's natural temperament strengths if you need help.) Then, use the cards to pray for your spouse every day and to thank God for how he or she is wonderfully made in our Lord's image. Even if your marriage is in crisis and your spouse is exhibiting weaknesses, do your best to focus on his or her positive qualities.

2. Verbally compliment your spouse. Tell your spouse what you like about him or her. Don't force this, just do it in conversation as the Lord leads you. Also tell others what you like about your spouse. This may seem difficult if you are in severe crisis because it is so opposite of what people expect to hear when couples aren't getting along. But that is exactly why it is so powerful. Satan wants you to speak negative things about each other so that he can cause division. But God will use your words of blessing on your spouse to release supernatural power. Regardless of what your spouse is doing, your part is to obey God. "And this is his command: to believe in the name of his Son, Jesus Christ, and to love one another as he commanded us. Those who obey his commands live in him, and he in them" (1 John 3:23-24).

When people are appreciated for their differences rather than judged, they will feel loved and understood. Consequently, a spouse or family member who is authentically complimented will exhibit strengths more readily and feel secure in the marriage and family. Can you think of a teacher, boss, or parent who believed in you and focused on your abilities rather than your shortcomings? More than likely, you excelled when you were in this person's presence because you felt appreciated and confident. The Bible is filled with scriptures that tells us to treat others with love and respect. The apostle Paul certainly understood the importance of it: "Do not let any unwholesome talk come out of your mouths, but only what is helpful for building others up according to their needs" (Ephesians 4:29).

3. Avoid pointing out your spouse's weaknesses. When people are criticized or judged regularly, they will feel unloved. As Dr. Carbonell said, this causes them to lean on their natural strengths for survival—usually to the extreme—and their strengths will then become their weaknesses. People with perfectionistic temperaments tend to be more critical of others (as well as themselves), but any temperament can fall into this habit. When you focus on your spouse's or children's weaknesses, it becomes a vicious cycle: Your spouse or children feel unloved, so they act out in an unloving way; then, because they exhibit their weaknesses rather than their strengths, you become critical, focusing on their negative behavior, and on it goes. One relationship counselor, Dr. Robert Ross, refers to this as the "phenomenon of reactivity." He says, "This is a circular pattern in which each spouse 'helps' the other maintain his or her negative behavior. For example: the husband neglects his wife and doesn't spend time with her, so she nags, so he neglects her, and so on."

4. Choose to live in balance. Jesus was the perfect blend of all four temperaments: His first miracle took place at a party (Sanguine); He was a powerful leader, focused on the goal He was here to accomplish, and He stood up to the religious leaders of His day (Choleric); He cared about every detail and fulfilled the law of the Old Testament (Melancholy); and, He was the Prince of Peace, focused on the most important character quality of a Christian: love (Phlegmatic). As Christians, we have access to the perfect blend of all four temperaments through the Holy Spirit, but we have to *choose* to live in the Spirit nature rather than our fleshly nature. We need to be balanced.

The best way to do this is to study the strengths of each of the temperaments and work on implementing those strengths in your life. This takes practice, but it isn't as difficult as you might think. For example, if you scored low in Melancholy and aren't a detailed person by nature, practice taking time on a project and ask a Melancholy friend to help give you pointers on becoming a more detailed person. If you scored low in Sanguine, force yourself to go to a party sometime and meet new people, or give up a day of scheduled activities just so you can be spontaneous. Learning to be balanced is not only fun, but it is also expected of us as we mature and become more Christlike.

5. Make deposits into your spouse's emotional love tank. Keeping your spouse's emotional love tank full is just as important as filling up your *spiritual fuel tank* (discussed in chapter 3). If your spouse thinks you don't love him or her, it will be just as destructive to your relationship as if you were to focus on his or her weaknesses and be critical all the time. Your spouse's behavior will change because he or she feels unloved, which will bring out the worst in his or her natural temperament. Author and marriage counselor Gary Chapman says that people behave differently when their emotional love tanks are full: "I am convinced that keeping the emotional love tank full is as important to a marriage as maintaining the proper oil level is to an automobile. Running your marriage on an empty 'love tank' may cost you even more than trying to drive your car without oil . . . people behave differently when their emotional love tanks are full." [5]

6. Know your spouse's "love language." Keeping your spouse's love tank full isn't as easy as you might think. Did you know it's possible for you to love your spouse, yet have them believe that you don't? According to Gary Chapman's book *The Five Love Languages,* there are five common methods of expressing love, and all of us have one method we consider our primary love language. He says, "If we want (a loved one) to feel the love we are trying to communicate, we must express it in his or her primary love language." [6] The five possible languages include:

1. Words of Affirmation: A person feels most loved when given compliments and kind words.
2. Quality Time: A person feels most loved with face-to-face communication and one-on-one time.
3. Acts of Service: A person feels most loved when people do acts of kindness for him or her, such as helping around the house, etc.

4. Physical Touch: A person feels most loved with hugs and touches but not necessarily sexual touch.
5. Receiving Gifts: A person feels most loved when receiving gifts on special or random occasions.

Everyone shows and receives love through all five love languages, but remember that only one will be dominant. If you have never studied the love languages, it would be helpful for you to get Chapman's book and have your whole family take the test. Joe's primary language is giving and receiving gifts. For years, every time he bought me something, he thought he was saying, "I love you," but my primary love language is words of affirmation, and when I wanted to tell Joe I loved him, I just said so. I didn't buy him gifts. Neither of us heard the other one expressing love because we were speaking different love languages.

Now that we know our primary love languages, we make sure that we speak those to each other, especially on birthdays and special occasions. When we realized what our love languages were, Joe jokingly said, "If I had known all you wanted was a card and dinner together on your birthday, I could have saved thousands of dollars over the years!" (I was quick to remind him that receiving "gifts" is my third choice of expression.) Both of our secondary choices of expression are quality time, which is why we have been able to work together side by side all these years.

In the case of one couple whose marriage was in crisis, when the husband learned his wife's love language, it made a huge difference: "When my wife and I learned about the different love languages, it saved our marriage. I had been traveling a lot in my job and I would buy Karen things, call her when I was gone, and constantly tell her I loved her. But she kept telling me she felt unloved. I couldn't understand it because I really loved her and I thought I was showing her. When we took the love language test in Gary Chapman's book, I discovered that her primary love language was quality time. Since I traveled, it didn't matter how much I said the words or how many gifts I gave her—she felt unloved because I wasn't physically with her. My primary love language is words of affirmation, so Karen could have kept my love tank filled with cards and phone calls (which she started doing more of after we took the test). I know there are couples who have spouses that travel and are able to have great marriages, but for us it nearly destroyed our marriage. I changed jobs so I could be home and immediately Karen felt the love she had been missing. We made a few other changes too, but giving Karen the quality time she needed is what really turned our marriage around."

7. *Learn to "complete" rather than "compete."* In the past few years, there have been numerous books, both Christian and secular, that explain the differences between men and women and how to accept these differences. We are drawn to our spouses in a desire to complete each other. In their book, *Men Are Like Waffles—Women Are Like Spaghetti,* Bill and Pam Farrel write:

> As research accumulates, it is becoming increasingly obvious that God made men and women different in many ways. They think differently, they process emotions differently, they make decisions differently, and they learn differently. And yet men and women complement one another so beautifully that a healthy relationship makes both partners more complete.[7]

Because of the differing needs of men and women, this can be a huge source of conflict. In his book *What Men Want,* H. Norman Wright pens an imaginary dialogue with God about Adam and Eve. At one point God says: "A relationship that was meant to be complimentary became competitive. Eve's desire was to control Adam. . . . The mutual security and love they shared in each other's presence was first tarnished, then it was broken. . . . The result has been a power struggle. Man's strength became perverted; and his perverted sense of strength led to domination rather than loving leadership in marriage. . . ."[8]

I (Michelle) hear women say all the time that if their husbands would just be more loving, they would feel like being more romantic. But according to most relationship experts, women need to set the mood by being romantic *first*, then their husbands will be more loving (the "reactivity" theory mentioned earlier).

Men typically have a harder time expressing their feelings, which makes it difficult for their wives to know what they need. Most women, on the other hand, usually share their feelings openly, but have learned from experience that when they do so, their husbands try to solve the problem rather than listen. H. Norman Wright describes a "wise man" this way: "A man who has learned not to offer solutions . . . or downplay his wife's problems . . . has arrived. He is now wise."[9]

Even with prayer, trying to understand one another is nearly impossible because men and women are created to be different and only God truly understands how He created us. The Farrels agree: "We have been told numerous times that true intimacy is attained when a couple understands one another. The problem is that a man will never fully understand a woman and a woman will never fully understand a man."[10]

I (Joe) have a book in our office that I hand to guys when they start complaining about not being able to understand their wives. The title is *Everything Men Know About Women*, and when you open it, all 200 pages are blank. There was a reason I picked up that book when I saw the cover—I wanted to know too. The other thing I tell the guys is that there are two times in a couple's life that they won't understand each other: before the wedding and after the wedding. But that doesn't mean we can't go to the One who *does* understand us—and the One who made us—in order to better understand our spouses.

8. *Meet each other's needs.* Most relationship experts agree that men's and women's needs are different. Based on our own needs and from an informal survey we have been doing for years, we have come up with six of the most common needs of men and women in marriage:

A man needs (1) respect and admiration (honest communication, but not argumentative behavior regarding his ideas and decisions); (2) a wife who desires him sexually; (3) a spouse who takes care of herself physically; (4) domestic support (a wife who backs his decisions and keeps the home orderly); (5) down time to relax (usually in front of a television, since it doesn't require him to make decisions); and (6) activities (playing sports, watching sports, etc.).

A woman needs (1) a husband who is a man of character and who is loyal and lovingly protects her; (2) affection (not sexual; however, most women have shared that when these six needs are met, they *do* desire their husbands sexually); (3) face-to-face conversation (that's why going out to dinner is so romantic when dating); (4) honesty (one little lie can destroy her ability to be intimate); (5) financial security (most women have told us that they would give up a "big house and material wealth" for a man who exhibited the first four qualities on this list); and (6) family commitment (spending quality time with children and doing things as a family).

With such different needs and different methods of meeting those needs, is it any wonder men and women have trouble keeping each other's emotional love tanks filled? Even so, God doesn't let that be a reason to ignore His command for husbands and wives to "submit to one another out of reverence for Christ. Wives, submit to your husbands as to the Lord. For the husband is head of the wife as Christ is the head of the church, his body, of which he is the Savior. Husbands, love your wives, just as Christ loved the church and gave himself up for her" (Ephesians 5:21-23, 25). We need to do our best to meet the needs of one another out of our love for Christ.

Other Unique Differences

Over the years, we have discovered that not everyone will identify with his or her temperament or love language test results. And most relationship experts agree that about 20 percent of people don't fit the norm in the differences between men and women. We have also come to realize that some people just don't like being labeled. It makes them feel like their individuality has been stripped away. Still, almost everyone agrees that there are other unique differences in all of us that affect how we relate to one another. Here are the six we see most commonly:

1. Childhood experience differences. Since no two people were raised exactly the same, each of us enters marriage with our own unique lens of experiences, and that lens works as a filter for new experiences. Here are some experiences that may affect how you (or your spouse) view life:

- If you were raised in a two-parent home vs. a single-parent home
- If your parents are divorced
- If one or both of your parents had an addiction of some kind
- If there was sexual or physical abuse in your family
- Your religious experience
- Ethnic and cultural differences
- Heredity issues affecting your health or ability to bear children
- Your financial background

2. Spiritual differences. The spiritual differences between you and your spouse can be a huge factor in your marriage. This is especially difficult if one of you is a believer and the other isn't because a Christian has the power of Christ living in them through the Holy Spirit and a nonbeliever doesn't. Even in cases where both spouses are believers, one is usually more mature spiritually than the other and, as a result, the more mature Christian will have to guard against the desire to "play God" in his or her spouse's life. One lady told us, "I used to try to correct my husband when I thought he wasn't acting very spiritually mature, but that always made things worse. Then, I discovered if I kept my mouth shut that God could get to him better than I ever could. Now, instead of correcting him, I just move aside for the Holy Spirit and let God do the work. It's amazing how much my husband has grown in the Lord since I moved out of the way!"

3. Energy-level differences. No husband and wife have the same energy level. To expect your spouse to keep up or shut down physically at the same rate you do is to set yourself up for pressure in your marriage. When a couple is dating, they both seem to have endless energy trying to balance work and fun and still have time to talk for hours before the day is over. However, after the wedding, when the couple begins getting into a regular routine, there will probably be a natural preference and difference in bedtime routines. Most of the couples we know have had to come to a compromise in this area. One woman told us, "I have more energy late at night, but my husband gets tired early. So, I go to bed with him when he's ready, and then after he's asleep I will often get up and write until two or three in the morning."

4. Health differences. All of us will suffer illness at one time or another and our bodies will all age differently. Some individuals may even have to rearrange their whole lives because of a spouse's health problems. If your spouse has been diagnosed with a chronic illness or disease that will affect him or her for life, it will be difficult to give up the activities you once shared as a couple, but accepting this difference and facing it with compassion can bring a new sense of unity to your marriage. We have met several couples over the years who have grown closer as a result of coming alongside an ailing or aging spouse in love.

One woman shared: "When I hurt my back in a skiing accident, my husband had to rearrange his whole life. We were young and very athletic before the accident, and all of a sudden, I had to spend time practicing pain-management exercises instead of riding mountain bikes with him. But over the years, I have learned to deal with the pain and my husband has learned how to provide the compassion and comfort I need. Our lives changed, but we have grown closer in so many ways. We still enjoy hobbies together, but we've had to learn to rearrange things a bit. For example, when he goes on bike rides now, I spend that time writing. And we have also discovered several new common interests and hobbies so that we can still spend quality time together."

5. *Decision-making differences.* No two people make decisions exactly the same way, especially big ones such as having children, buying or furnishing a home, or changing jobs. Michelle shared, "When we first got married I had the hardest time with how Eric and I made decisions when it came to purchasing things for our home. One time, I saw a cabinet in a catalog that was exactly what we had been looking for, so I told Eric we needed to order it. I'm goal driven by nature and prior to getting married, when I wanted something I just went to the store and bought it—regardless of the price. Eric, on the other hand, likes to bargain hunt. He loves those off-the-wall places where you have to dig under piles of dusty items just to find what you're looking for. When I tried to get him to order the cabinet from the catalog, he said, 'Michelle, that takes the whole fun out of it. Just let me hunt for it. I can find it—name brand and all—and it will be fun.'

"I decided that ordering the cabinet wasn't worth an argument, and agreed to wait while he went on his search. To tell you the truth, I never really expected he would find it. But several weeks later there it was—in the back of a consignment shop! It was exactly like the one in the catalog and looked brand new. When I questioned him as to why it was less than half the price of a new one, he showed me a little tiny nick on the bottom corner that no one could even see. That day I made up my mind not to let our decision-making differences be a source of conflict. I'm glad too, because over the years we've gotten some pretty good bargains, and we've had so much fun searching for them together."

6. *Family-of-origin differences.* Neither you nor your spouse will ever be able to change your family of origin or your childhood experiences. A lot of your reactions and the filter that you see experiences through come from the way you were raised. Nevertheless, you must learn to accept and integrate your differences or it can be a huge source of conflict after you marry, and, especially after you become parents. We have read several books over the years that describe different types of families. There seems to be five that are most common:

1. The Overprotective Family: The parents in this family hover over their children, never allowing them to take on age-appropriate responsibilities. As a result, the children are not able to develop their own sense of confidence. However, the positive aspect of this family is that the children do feel loved and cared for.

2. The Disconnected Family: The members of this family feel disengaged from one another. Everyone looks out for their own interests. Sometimes the children are neglected or abused. However, the children do learn to be self-sufficient.

3. The Conforming Family: In this family, individuality is viewed as an offense. Children are made to feel guilty when they don't conform to the ideals of the family as a whole. They feel accepted when embracing the same political and religious views as their parents. These children usually grow up with some great traditions.

4. The Dictator Family: The parents in this family tend to push their authority on their children and they can be insensitive or abrasive. The children will often feel unloved. These children tend to grow up with an understanding of rules.

5. The Connected Family: This family, of course, is the model of balance between all four. They are not threatened by differences and everyone is encouraged to be all he or she can be.

To become a more connected family, study the positive aspects from each of the other four descriptions and do your best to begin implementing them into your own family now. This will be more challenging if you or your spouse had a lot of negative experiences in your family of origin, but with the power of God and your sincere desire to make changes, it is never too late.

∾

If you have never discussed the topics covered in this chapter with your spouse, pray for an opportunity to do so. We have found that if one spouse begins the discussion by being vulnerable first, oftentimes the other spouse will contribute to the conversation. The key is to give your spouse the opportunity without being demanding.

We heard a Christian speaker once say, "Become a student of your spouse . . . learn about him or her." That's what we want to encourage you to do as you implement the tools in this chapter in your life. Spend time getting to know your spouse and children and then focus on the positive things about them and let the negative ones go. You will never fully understand those you love, but with God's help, you can try.

GROUP OR SUPPORT-PARTNER DISCUSSION QUESTIONS

1. *According to your scores on pages 69-70, what is your basic temperament?*
2. *What do you think your main love language is?*
3. *What is your family of origin?*

4. *What do you think the basic temperaments and love languages of your spouse and children are?*

5. *Look up and discuss Ephesians 4:1-16.*

6. *What positive qualities in your spouse are you grateful to God for?*

7. *What weaknesses in your own temperament do you need prayer for?*

Anger Can Be Handled God's Way

Never take your own revenge, beloved, but leave room for
the wrath of God, for it is written, "Vengence is mine, I
will repay," says the Lord.

—ROMANS 12:19, NASB

"Joe, you make me so angry, I just can't take it anymore!"
Stomping up the stairs, I ran into the bathroom and
slammed the door. I looked for something to throw but instead
punched my fist through the lid of an unsuspecting wicker basket. My
predicament would have been funny if it weren't so painful: My arm
had gone through the lid of the basket up to the elbow where the
wicker teeth were positioned for revenge. After taking a deep breath
and pulling free, I opened one eye to survey the damage. Blood was
oozing from several deep claw marks in my arm.

A couple of days later I attended an overnight conference with several friends from work, and it was impossible to hide the gouge marks
in my arm. My friends got a good laugh out of the "revenge-of-the-
wicker-basket" episode, but as far as I was concerned, I knew God did
not look favorably on what I had done. This incident occurred during
our second separation. Just after the event I rededicated my life to

Christ, but the scabs served as a constant reminder that I had a lot of changes to make in the area of anger.

I was raised in a family that held nothing back when it came to expressing anger. All I had ever witnessed when it came to dealing with conflict was yelling, cursing, hitting, and/or throwing things—even to the point of breaking valuables or ripping up clothing. In my family, whoever yelled the loudest, was most aggressive, or most vindictive, emerged the winner.

I really wanted to turn over a new leaf as a follower of Christ, especially in the area of anger, so I repented and vowed to God to make a change. With practiced attempts to remain calm, the anger stopped—*or so it seemed*. Because my anger had ceased and Joe had become a Christian, I thought we were on our way to finally having a good marriage. It was during this "peaceful" time that we renewed our marriage vows in November of 1986.

The first few weeks back together were pretty calm. But every time we had the slightest disagreement, instead of working it through we would quickly end the discussion to avoid any possibility of our anger escalating out of control. What we didn't realize was that we were just suppressing our anger. With so much unresolved conflict buried, small eruptions began to occur. It was at that time I admitted to our home-fellowship group at church that our marriage was once again in crisis. It was in the midst of a heated argument that we separated for the last time. We both unloaded months of pent-up anger, and I shattered an entire stack of dishes.

For the next five years—even after we reconciled and started serving in ministry together—Joe and I struggled with how to handle our anger God's way. We mistakenly believed Christians were not supposed to get angry. Consequently, we tried to ignore the emotion and bury it every time it surfaced. But we could suppress it for only so long before one of us would erupt or stomp off in a fit of rage. After we cooled off, we would make up, but the destructive cycle would soon begin again. As time went on our eruptions happened less frequently, but they still happened and we both knew we weren't dealing with our anger appropriately.

The more we studied the Bible and matured in our Christian walks, the more determined we became to stop our anger outbursts. We read books, took classes, and studied God's Word searching for answers. We did our best to apply everything we learned, but we continued to have problems with expressing anger in healthy ways. After lots of study and research, we discovered that we'd had a misconception about anger all along: Anger isn't a sin; anger is an emotion given to us by God for a purpose. We had never considered the emotion of anger as a warning signal to help us. Instead, we viewed anger as a monster waiting to devour our marriage.

We also learned the emotional pain of anger would work much like physical pain: Ignoring it would be just as detrimental to the health of our marriage as ignoring the physical pain of touching a hot stove. By suppressing our anger, we were ignoring a warning signal that something was wrong.

The misconception that couples will have better marriages if they simply *avoid* conflict often leads to more serious problems like suppressing anger and blocking intimacy. We have learned over the years that God uses conflict to grow us closer to Him as well as closer to each other. To pretend we weren't angry when we were was just as sinful in God's eyes as shouting or breaking something. By pretending, we were being dishonest.

In his book *Sacred Marriage*, Gary Thomas calls this "polite pretending" and writes, "Mature adults realize that every relationship involves conflict, confession, and forgiveness. Unless you truly enjoy hanging around a sycophant (phony flatterer), the absence of conflict demonstrates that either the relationship isn't important enough to fight over or that both individuals are too insecure to risk disagreement."[1]

〜◎〜

Once Michelle and I stopped fearing the emotion of anger and viewed it as an emotion given to us by God, we were able to start making positive, lasting changes, but not without a lot of work. One thing we continued to struggle with even after viewing anger as our ally was how to apply Ephesians 4:26: "Do not let the sun go down while you are still angry." Like many Christians, we thought this verse meant that every disagreement had to be resolved before we went to sleep.

This was difficult for us because our biggest arguments always seemed to occur in the evenings. There were many times when one or both of us pretended our anger was gone just to get some sleep. But with our tendency to bury issues rather than resolve them, pretending we weren't angry trapped us in our suppress-and-erupt cycle.

Finally, as we studied Ephesians 4:26 in context with the sur-rounding scriptures, we discovered God gave us the solution for deal-ing with anger: "You were taught, with regard to your former way of life, to put off your old self, which is being corrupted by its deceitful desires; to be made new in the attitude of your minds; and to put on the new self, created to be like God in true righteousness and holiness" (Ephesians 4:22-24).

Our natural tendency was to suppress our anger or pretend it didn't exist. But God revealed His supernatural solution to us through this verse: "Therefore, each of you must put off falsehood and speak truthfully to his neighbor, for we are all members of one body. In your anger do not sin. Do not let the sun go down while you are still angry, and do not give the devil a foothold" (Ephesians 4:25-27).

Take Off All Falsehood

Joe and I studied these verses together because we wanted to help others with their anger as well as make changes in our own lives. Because we would be teaching on the subject of anger, it forced us to dig deeper than we might normally have done. What we learned was that as long as we avoided dealing with issues as they came up, we would never be able to express anger in a way that was pleasing to God. Paul wants Christians to understand our old way of life was deceitfulness, but now as followers of Christ we are to speak the truth (always in love, of course). In doing so, the Devil will not be able to get a foothold in our anger.

Practically speaking, if you and your spouse have an argument some evening and you can see that it is not going to be resolved soon, you may have to say something like, "You know, I'm getting tired and you must be too. Let's get some sleep and bring this up later after we've had time to rest and pray and can think clearly." By doing this, you are speaking truth in love.

If your spouse accuses you of still being upset—*and you are*—admit it. Simply say something like, "You know, feeling anger isn't a sin, but lying to you right now would be. Yes, I'm still upset and that's even more reason why we shouldn't try to discuss this late into the night. I love you and am committed to this marriage, but now I need to get some sleep."

Maybe you are thinking, *Are you kidding? My spouse would follow me around the house and demand we resolve the argument!* or *There's no way I would ever let my spouse go off to bed like that. I would make him/her stay up to settle our problem—especially if my spouse admitted to still being upset!* If those are your thoughts right now, then there is a deeper issue going on in your home: control and boundary problems. (We will discuss boundaries in chapter 8. For now, do what you can to apply the tools in this chapter.)

One thing that we found most helpful in our search for dealing with anger constructively and taking off falsehood with each other was to understand why people feel the emotion of anger to begin with. Most of the books we have read listed basic reasons, but the following four rise to the top of the list:

1. *Hurt* due to damaging words or actions or physical pain due to bodily injury.

2. *Frustration* because someone isn't complying with our needs or expectations or the frustration of losing something or when equipment or technology is not working properly.

3. *Fear* of losing someone's love or fear for our physical safety.

4. *Injustice* from disappointed expectation of fairness or righteous anger resulting from the mistreatment of others.

After thinking of anger as a friendly warning and realizing that it was a secondary emotion to one of these four areas, I (Michelle) decided to spend a week or so tracking the emotion every time it surfaced. Instead of using the word *anger*, I used the words *hurt, frustrated, fearful,* or *unjust* (or a combination of them) in order to get to the root of the emotion. Then I practiced saying the reasons aloud, but not in an angry tone of voice. For instance, if something was misplaced I would say, "I'm really frustrated right now because of losing _____." In the case of hurt feelings because of something Joe said or did, I practiced saying, "That was a hurtful comment." It actually became fun to uncover some of the reasons I felt angry and to begin viewing the emotion of anger as an ally in our home. This exercise began to diffuse my anger because I was honestly identifying the source of it, exposing the truth behind each episode.

It was freeing to realize the emotion of anger is not a sin. We are made in God's image, and there are several hundred verses in the Bible that speak of the Lord's anger. God is clear in every passage that we are not to sin in our anger, but He never tells us that anger itself is a sin. On the contrary, the apostle Paul writes, "Be ye angry, and sin not" (Ephesians 4:26 KJV).

However, while the emotion of anger isn't a sin, we discovered the way we usually expressed it was. It is natural to sin in your anger when you are hurt, frustrated, fearful, or if there has been injustice. We are born with a selfish sin nature. Just watch any two-year-old react to another toddler taking away his toy. Thankfully, as Christians we have the Spirit of Christ dwelling in us to help us overcome our fleshly desires.

Do your best to practice self-control and accept God's grace when you fall. While we live on this earth, we will continue to war against our flesh and our spirit: "For the sinful nature desires what is contrary to the Spirit, and the Spirit what is contrary to the sinful nature. They are in conflict with each other, so that you do not do what you want" (Galatians 5:17).

The important thing to remember is that when you stumble or fall, repent quickly and reach out to God for forgiveness. He will always extend back to you another chance to get it right the next time.

Avoid Passive-Aggressive Behavior

One of the reasons—besides obeying God—that it's important to express anger as He intended is because not doing so may result in passive-aggressive anger. According to most psychologists and relationship experts, passive-aggressive anger is the most difficult behavior to deal with because the anger is unmanaged and the source is unidentified. If you or your spouse is angry but won't spend the energy or time to uncover the reason why, your marriage is in danger of being destroyed because of passive-aggressive behavior. Some signs of passive-aggressive anger are:

- Substance abuse
- Emotionally withdrawing from important relationships
- Adulterous affairs
- Lying
- Refusing to participate in family or couple-oriented events
- Withholding sex
- Refusing to communicate
- Secret sin such as pornography or inappropriate Internet use

Satan likes to sidetrack couples with sinful behavior instead of allowing them to deal with the real issues causing their anger because he doesn't want strong marriages. Satan wants marriages based on deception, but God wants marriages based on truth.

~∽⊚∿~

I (Joe) like to use the example of a hand grenade when teaching others about anger. I use an old diffused hand grenade, mounted like a trophy. I call it an "anger-nade." We are all potential anger-nades if we are not expressing our anger God's way by exposing it to the light. If we are stuffing it and pretending it's not there, someone's liable to come along and innocently pull our "pin," and the explosion can cause irreparable damage to those we care about most. I have talked with men who lost their whole families because of their anger explosions. I tell them they must "learn to diffuse, to be used." I instruct them to blow up a balloon with their hot air and pop it the next time they start getting all bent out of shape about something. It helps them release some of their frustration and gives them time to process their next step.

Another thing that can help diffuse anger is humor. When Michelle and I can find humor in a situation that is becoming stressful, it allows us to relax a little and not take the situation too seriously. We accidentally discovered this tool when a situation arose many years ago that was very frustrating. Normally this situation would have resulted in one or both of us getting angry. This time, because it resulted in laughter, we realized the power of humor in stressful situations.

When our son, Mick, was young, we had a hard time buying clothes for him. Everything seemed to bug him—socks, shirts, pants, you name it. Whenever we had to take him shopping we both dreaded it, and neither one of us wanted to do it alone. By the time we got home usually one or both of us were irritated and worn out from the experience. One night, during one of these dreaded shopping trips, Michelle and I were standing outside the dressing-room door in a clothing store catching the pairs of pants our son was hurling over the top. We were getting frustrated listening to our son complaining, "These pants don't fit either!" as another pair flew over the door. Then I noticed that he had thrown his own pants at us—the ones he wore into the store—saying *they* didn't fit. It was so funny when we discovered he had tried his own pants on, not realizing it, and decided they didn't fit either, that Michelle and I couldn't stop laughing. We weren't angry anymore because the laughter and humor had diffused our frustration and we were able to see our situation clearly. It even changed how our son was behaving. While he tried not to laugh, he ended up giving in to the humor; we still laugh about it today, 12 years later.

Let God Bless You

Eventually, I (Michelle) was able to put into practice much of what I learned and had shared with others concerning anger. Every now and then, however, I would fall back into the old behavior and start suppressing and exploding to express my anger. But I continued to repent and ask God for help. Finally, one day while Joe and I were having an argument, the Lord revealed something that changed the way I dealt with anger once and for all. When our argument began to look like it wasn't going to be resolved quickly, I started to clam up and walk away. This time, however, I sensed the Lord saying, "If you pass this test and express your anger the way I want you to—by bringing it into the light and fearing Me rather than Joe—a blessing awaits."

I decided to step out in obedience to the Lord, take off all falsehood (no matter how angry Joe became), and not sin in expressing my anger. That revelation was truly a turning point and the "blessing" of God came quickly. Instead of stomping off, I faced Joe and spoke truth, remaining focused on the issue at hand—even though he was visibly frustrated. Our argument was completely resolved in a way that honored God and each other. The "blessing" that awaited was the intimacy between us because the issue was completely resolved and I did not fall back into my old patterns of behavior. I experienced the same confidence most of us relate to the first time we learn how to ride a bike: I "got it," and even if I fell off the bike, I finally knew how to ride one.

Until that moment, unresolved issues had remained buried in our relationship, evidenced by our explosions when tensions were high. Unresolved issues caused a crescendo of stress: When a new problem arose, we didn't have the strength in our relationship to deal with it as a stand-alone issue. Instead of staying focused on the problem that needed to be resolved, the focus always shifted to how one of us was sinning in our anger.

～ఞ〜

This was a huge turning point in our marriage. When Michelle stopped having those anger explosions or walking away and shutting me out emotionally, it took about a year to finally believe she had changed. I kept waiting for her old behavior to come back. Sometimes I would even say, "Okay, here it comes . . . go ahead and blow up. . . ." Saying something like that would have been like pulling the pin on the "anger-nade" in the past. It wasn't that I wanted her to explode; I just wanted to get it over with because I thought it was coming anyway. But because we had started dealing with issues as they came up, the bomb wasn't there anymore. Because she was focusing her anger on the source of the problem, it forced me to do the same and over time, I changed too.

Anger Expressions Are Learned

Experts agree that we learn how to express anger by what is modeled to us as children. It is never too late to change the way you express your anger—even if your spouse refuses to do so. Learning to express anger by identifying its source will model to your spouse and your children how to avoid passive-aggressive behavior. Our children were almost grown by the time we finally got a handle on our anger, but by the grace of God, we have since modeled our new behavior and displayed the correct way anger should be expressed.

In their book *The Five Love Languages of Children*, Gary Chapman and Ross Campbell write: "Remember, all anger must come out either verbally or behaviorally. If you don't allow it to come verbally, passive-aggressive behavior will follow." [2]

Using an example of how Campbell helped his son, David, to verbally express anger, he writes: "Another reason I wanted the anger to (verbally) come out was that as long as it was inside of David, it controlled the house. . . . The more anger he expressed verbally, the less there would be to come out in lying, stealing, sex, drugs, and all the other passive-aggressive behaviors that are so common today." [3] (You can read more about kids dealing with anger in Ross Campbell's book *Kids in Danger*.)

STEPS TO GETTING TO THE ROOT OF ANGER

Since the emotion of anger is a secondary emotion, getting to the root of why the emotion is there in the first place is necessary in order to avoid "polite pretending." Sometimes the reason is a simple one and the issue is dealt with quickly. Other times, it's not so easy and takes some effort to uncover. These four steps can help you get to the root:

1. Admit self-centeredness. Most anger comes from not getting something that you want or think you need. Ask God to reveal any selfish attitudes. For example, if you are angry because you are frustrated with someone, ask God if your frustration is due to controlling demands or unrealistic expectations on your part. Or, if you're angry because you are hurt, ask God to show you if you have been overly sensitive and maybe even enjoying your "pity party."

"What causes fights and quarrels among you? Don't they come from your desires that battle within you? You want something but don't get it. You kill and covet, but you cannot have what you want. You quarrel and fight. You do not have because you do not ask God. When you ask, you do not receive, because you ask with wrong motives, that you may spend what you get on your pleasures" (James 4:1-3).

More often than not, by the time you have asked God to reveal your own self-centeredness in your anger, you won't even have to move on to the next step. Once you have confessed the truth to God—and to others if you are prompted to do so—the anger will have probably already subsided.

2. Be patient. There is a lot to be said for counting to 10 when you are angry. If you are still feeling angry after step one, then ask God to give you the patience you need while waiting for Him to reveal the root of your anger. Don't rush. Waiting and praying is by no means a passive behavior, but rather an effective way of allowing the truth and reasons for your anger to surface. Waiting in prayer also allows God to convict your heart of sin.

In our marriage, waiting before responding in anger has produced positive results in almost every disagreement we've had. Waiting also gives others who are part of the solution an opportunity to take responsibility for their actions.

3. *Respond to your situation in God's timing.* Sometimes you will have to take action to resolve the situation that is causing your anger. One thing we have noticed is that whatever our first inclination might be to solve the problem, after we pray and wait, God will usually require us to do the opposite. For instance, if my (Michelle) first inclination is to call and make an appointment with someone who has treated me or someone else unfairly, after I pray and wait, God will usually require that I overlook the offense. On the other hand, at times when my first inclination has been to be silent and overlook an injustice, after praying and waiting, God will usually stretch me by having me set up a Matthew 18 appointment (see Matthew 18:15-17).

For reasons such as these, it's important to practice these steps, so you don't rush into your response prematurely. You may need to gain perspective through counsel from others, or take time to evaluate your choices in order to resolve your conflict. This is another reason it is important to have a godly support system in place.

4. *Don't allow your anger or your spouse's to become a smoke screen to the real issue.* Family counselors often say that the runaway teen in a "perfect family" is the barometer they use to treat the family as a whole. Likewise, sometimes it is difficult to uncover the source of anger because one spouse's expression has become the main focus, rather than their issues as a couple. Here are two examples where one spouse's anger had become the smokescreen for their real issues:

"We hadn't even been married a month when my wife had her first 'tantrum' and threw her makeup at me. When it spilled all over our new carpet, I was livid. Allison definitely has an anger problem," Jim said, confident that if his wife changed, they would have a good marriage.

With an expression of sadness in her eyes, Allison responded: "When I threw the makeup at Jim, I realized I'd crossed the line. After apologizing and cleaning it up, I promised never to get that angry again. But when he hurts my feelings with his critical words, I end up blowing up and usually throwing something, saying things I regret, or even hitting him. I'm trying to avoid getting angry because it's taking such a toll on our marriage, but I just can't seem to stop blowing up."

In this couple's case they are both focused on Allison's anger because hers is the most obvious. They think if she can stop blowing up, they will have a better marriage. However, just because Jim is not throwing objects at Allison, his behavior is still sin. Her "tantrums" and his belittling words are secondary to what is really going on inside their hearts.

Through counseling, this couple discovered that Allison had deep wounds from childhood abuse and every time Jim said hurtful words, it brought up the abuse all over again. They also learned that the root of Jim's anger was that he felt disrespected by Allison because she questioned his decisions—especially in front of their children—and overrode his authority in the home because she was afraid to trust him. By getting to the root causes of their anger, they were able to work on the real issues in their marriage instead of focusing on Allison's tantrums.

In Victor and Cheryle's marriage, Victor's rage was the smoke screen. "I don't get angry, but Victor does," Cheryle explained in a quiet voice and with a sweet expression on her face. "He yells and stomps around the house like a charging bull. His nose flairs and you can almost see the steam coming out of his ears. When I cry and ask him to stop being so mean, he just huffs and puffs all the more. I don't understand how he can be so mean. I'm not mean to him."

Cheryle's sweet smile makes you think she is a sweet, loving person who would never hurt a flea. But Victor says otherwise: "She goes around my back telling our pastor and my family that I'm a monster and an alcoholic and that I've even behaved inappropriately with young girls! I may rage when I'm angry—and that's why I'm getting counseling—but all that other stuff is completely false. How can I stop raging if she doesn't stop lying to others about me?"

Because the focus is on Victor's aggressive behavior (notice he's the only one in counseling) this couple is missing an opportunity to deal with the underlying problems in their relationship. Cheryle doesn't think she's angry because she doesn't express it the same way Victor does. But her behavior is just as sinful in God's eyes, and her refusal to admit her sin is keeping this couple from reconciling.

HELP YOUR SPOUSE GET TO THE ROOT

Maybe, like Jim and Allison, you and your spouse are both willing to take responsibility for the anger issues in your marriage. But if your spouse is like Cheryle and refuses to work on the "log in her own eye" (Matthew 7), there are things you can do to help. If you behave like Victor, however, and continue allowing your unwilling spouse to control how you express your anger, you will never be able to make changes in your marriage.

1. Pray for your spouse. If you've had an opportunity to discuss the tools in this chapter with your spouse, make a list of the areas that he or she has admitted are a struggle. You already know the obvious areas you can pray for, but you might be surprised at the things your spouse will share if you just ask with a soft heart and honest motives.

2. Refill an empty "love tank." If your spouse's primary love language is acts of service, and he or she is feeling unloved, your spouse may angrily complain, "I never have any clean socks anymore" or "You used to check the water and oil in my car—but now you're too busy!" Likewise, a spouse feeling unloved whose love language is quality time may mumble, "You're always on the phone!" or "You're never home anymore!"

Remember also, that men and women are wired differently. Many experts agree that when dealing with stress and conflict, most men find sex and sleep as their favorite coping mechanisms, and most women need conversation as theirs. Bill and Pam Farrel write, "It is not difficult to see that this could cause trouble for the couple who does not have a deliberate plan to relieve stress . . . she wants conversation while he wants a safe retreat, or better yet to have sex before taking a nap!"[4]

3. Ask questions. If you notice that your spouse gets angry over trivial matters, but you have been trying to fill his or her love tank and the situation is not getting better, it's probably time to ask some honest questions. This will take a risk on your part, but remember that unless your spouse takes off all falsehood, the Devil will have a foothold on his or her anger. Pray for the right timing and avoid these types of discussions if either of you is tired, sick, or hungry. A word of caution: Avoid asking a lot of questions at once or in an interrogating manner. Consider working them into normal conversation when in the car, going on a walk, or while on a date. As difficult as it might be for your particular temperament, do not try to fix or solve your spouse's problem(s) unless you are asked to give advice. Doing so will send the message that you don't think your spouse is smart enough to figure out his or her own solution(s). Here are some questions you might consider asking:

- Is there anything at home or work that is frustrating right now?

- Do you feel disappointed or hurt over something at home or work?
- Has there been any type of injustice at work or home that you want to talk about?
- What do you fear most right now?

4. Listen. This is the most difficult, yet the most important part of this exercise. If your spouse has bottled-up anger, he or she may have to sift through some unrelated issues in order to identify the truth behind the current struggle. Some of those issues may even have to do with you. You will have to pray and guard against being defensive or sinning in your anger if your spouse says something hurtful. Remember, this is an opportunity to help your spouse place his or her anger in the light. Try to keep the conversation moving along, ask for clarification, remain calm, and help your spouse to uncover the source of his or her anger so that resolution can begin to take place. Avoid arguing at all cost. This is a time to listen to your spouse's fears, frustrations, hurts, or injustices. Once your spouse feels safe, he or she will take a risk to discuss hidden emotions.

It may take several attempts before your spouse feels safe enough to discuss anger, or get to the root of why he or she is feeling angry. Do your best to keep the conversation moving, but if your spouse wants the conversation to end, then quietly and respectfully walk away. The Lord will honor your gentle spirit. This exercise has not only helped in our marriage, but also with our children and others struggling with anger.

5. Don't play God by nagging your spouse. Once I (Michelle) stopped exploding and started dealing with anger constructively, God convicted me of another sin: pride. As Joe said, he didn't trust the changes in our home and was still struggling, trying to learn how to express his anger constructively. As a result, I developed a smug sense of achievement rather than a humble attitude. Instead of helping Joe verbalize his feelings of fear, frustration, hurt, or injustice, I criticized him for expressing anger in an ungodly way. Instead of being Joe's helpmate, I was trying to be his Holy Spirit. When the Lord revealed what I was doing, the conviction was overwhelming. Moving out of the way and allowing God to discipline Joe was much more effective than trying to nag him into changing.

6. *Don't play God by rescuing your spouse.* The best thing to do in dealing with others who are sinning in their anger is to let the natural consequences of their behavior be their teacher. "No discipline seems pleasant at the time, but painful. Later on, however, it produces a harvest of righteousness and peace for those who have been trained by it" (Hebrews 12:11).

Sometimes, an angry spouse will experience consequences to behavior that will greatly affect you as well. In these cases, you may be tempted to rescue your spouse, if for no other reason than to avoid your own embarrassment or emotional pain. But if you try to take away natural consequences of someone's sinful behavior, you will only make things worse in the long run. "A hot-tempered man must pay the penalty; if you rescue him, you will have to do it again" (Proverbs 19:19). This was the case in Dena's situation.

Dennis was a pastor in a church in Oregon for 18 years before his problem with rage was revealed to the congregation. His wife, Dena, and his three daughters had learned to tiptoe around Dennis's anger at home, pretending everything was alright when they were around others. Several times in their 20-year marriage Dena wondered if she was doing the right thing by covering up his problem with anger, yet each time Dena considered exposing the truth about his rage she reasoned it might cost him his position in the church. "I didn't want to be the reason Dennis wasn't serving God," she admitted after the marriage ended. One night in a fit of rage, Dennis hit Dena and she finally called the police. The call, which Dena should have made the first time he was physical with her, resulted in his resignation as pastor and ultimately ended their marriage.

On the other hand, in Tom and Kim's case, bringing the truth out saved their marriage. Kim was on staff at her church. She and Tom had been married for almost 10 years when she finally admitted to one of her pastors that their marriage was in severe crisis. They attended church together, and Tom even helped out in men's ministry events, but at home he punished Kim with long periods of silence whenever he was angry with her. This time he had refused to speak to her face-to-face for almost two months, and his emotional abuse had taken its toll on her. Trying to keep Tom's behavior in the dark only made the situation worse. Once their pastor met with Tom and confronted his behavior, he and Kim were able to get help and they reconciled.

7. *Get the help you need and become proactive.* Some anger is a result of physical or mental illness (we discuss this more in chapter 8). If your anger or your spouse's anger is uncontrollable and you are unable to make positive changes by implementing the tools in this chapter, you may need to get outside help from health-care professionals. We know of several marriages where one spouse was diagnosed with a physical illness or mental disorder that required medication in order to stop destructive anger outbursts. The important thing to remember if this is the case in your marriage is to never allow it to keep your or your spouse's problem with anger in the dark. Get the help you need now, and learn to be proactive.

Even though Michelle and I don't have those volcanic-type eruptions of anger anymore, we can still find ourselves falling back into sinful expressions if we aren't careful. One thing that enables us to deal with new problems constructively is keeping a clean slate and avoiding extra tension. Making sure there are no other unresolved issues and no extra tension in our lives also makes it easier if we have to put an issue aside until the next day or until it can get fully resolved.

Here are the areas in our own lives that can create tension between us if they get out of balance. As you read, think about the areas in your marriage that, when out of balance, bring added stress into the home.

1. Finances. If I (Joe) am overly concerned about our finances, my fuse gets short and things that would not normally bother me can really become frustrating. We've learned to be proactive in this area and keep our finances in order and stay out of debt.

2. Time alone. One thing we have noticed about couples whose marriages are in crisis—and it is true for us as well—is that they have often lost a sense of themselves as individuals. Marriage troubles and everyday demands can replace the simple enjoyments in life. We guard against this by making sure we "self-nurture" and by reducing the demands we place on one another to meet the full gamut of each other's needs. We both have a "self-nurture" list that consists of 15-20 activities that we can do alone. These are not immoral, illegal, or expensive, and we do our best to incorporate at least five activities a week into our private schedules. At the top of both our lists is our quiet time with God each day (more on this tool in chapter 10).

3. Scheduling. I (Michelle) am responsible for keeping our calendar. We like to eat at home at least three nights a week and also have our children and grandchildren over once a week. This is important to both of us, and we are much happier if we stay balanced in this area. I've learned that when we get overbooked, we become tired and cranky and don't have enough energy to deal with new problems when they come up. Taking care of our health, eating right, and getting enough rest is something I have become proactive with over the years as well.

4. Intimacy. If we get too busy to take time for romance in our marriage, we will start bickering over little things. Authors Bill and Pam Farrel agree that couples who commit to meeting each others' sexual and emotional intimacy needs will have better marriages all the way around if they keep balanced in this area. "A couple who is in sync with each other sexually will be more confident, will think clearer, and will be more willing to sacrifice themselves for the good of the relationship." [5]

5. *Our home.* For me (Joe), when chores begin to pile up—the yard needs to be mowed and things around the house need to be fixed—I become frustrated. Michelle gets frustrated when her office or the dining room table gets cluttered. If just one of these areas is in disorder, it's not too stressful, but when several areas are ignored, the tension really begins to build.

6. *Fun.* We love to play games in the evenings after dinner. We have ongoing domino tournaments, and we play games with family members or friends on a regular basis. We also combine our self-nurture activities whenever possible and enjoy things together, like thrift-store shopping, yard sales, bike riding, or going for coffee.

∽⊘∾

We have given you tools in this chapter that have revolutionized our lives as well as our marriage. Over the years, others who have learned to use these tools tell us the same thing has happened for them. It is our prayer that as you begin to implement the tools in this chapter, your life and your marriage will be revolutionized as well. Here is a recap of what to do the next time you are angry:

1. Understand that anger is not a sin.
2. Accept the emotion of anger as your friend and a warning that you are hurt, frustrated, fearful, or dealing with injustice.
3. Take off all falsehood and admit what you are feeling.
4. Each time you sin in your anger, confess it to God and ask for His supernatural grace to help you do better next time.

One of the most important keys to expressing your anger God's way is honesty. If you don't know how to be honest in all circumstances, then you will not be able to take off falsehood.

GROUP OR SUPPORT-PARTNER
DISCUSSION QUESTIONS

1. *Based on the explanations as to why people feel the emotion of anger, what reasons tend to make you the most angry?*

2. *How do you usually express your anger?*

3. *Discuss the benefits of controlling your anger.*

4. *Discuss how "taking off all falsehood" can help you control your anger God's way.*

5. *Look up and discuss Hebrews 12:14-15.*

6. *Share something that you are especially grateful for this week.*

7. *Share a prayer request. Have you and your spouse had an opportunity to discuss the tools in this chapter and the previous one on temperaments? How are you praying for your spouse at this time?*

7

Even Little White Lies Are Big Trouble

The night is almost gone, and the day is near. Therefore let us lay aside the deeds of darkness and put on the armor of light.

—ROMANS 13:12 NASB

A few years after Joe and I were married, I made a huge mathematical error in our business account. Since our marriage was already on shaky ground, confessing that our checking account was overdrawn didn't seem like the wisest thing to do. In an attempt to avoid conflict, I devised a plan to borrow the money from my grandfather. *After all*, I schemed, *I don't have to tell Joe everything. And besides, this is one of those areas that qualifies as a "little white lie." Why tell Joe something that will only upset him? I can get the money paid back without ever having to bother him with this!*

My dance of deceit turned into a waltz of tangled webs before it finally ended in one of our biggest arguments. Several weeks after borrowing the money and paying it back, I discovered that there was some extra money in our account. That's when it became evident that I'd made an addition error. However, when I told Joe the whole story, instead of being happy that we had extra money, he became angry and accused me of deceitful behavior. When I tried to explain that my actions were designed to take unnecessary pressure off him (another lie), it only made matters worse. I didn't understand at the time that covering up to keep peace in our marriage was actually lying, and that God considers this kind of behavior a sin: "Do not lie to each other" (Colossians 3:9). It would be several years before God would finally get my full attention in the area of dishonesty.

I was reared in a home where respecting other people's feelings, needs, and desires was of great importance. Without the knowledge of God's Word, however, I learned it was all right to tell a little lie now and then to "help" a situation, or to keep those I loved from feeling sad or upset. When I rededicated my life to Christ and started attending church, I thought that kind of behavior was still applicable. Sadly, many Christians I encountered also justified lies or manipulated details for the sake of being "diplomatic" or keeping peace at all costs.

Once, a woman sitting next to me in a Bible study class casually said, "Tonight my daughter and I are going to see a movie that I saw two days ago, but I'll have to pretend it's the first time I've seen it." When I asked her why she would have to pretend she hadn't seen the movie, the woman explained she had promised her daughter they would see the movie together, and didn't want her daughter to be upset because she'd seen it with someone else first. Another time, a woman from church admitted she hid her cigarette smoking from her grown children. She had promised them she would give up the habit, but hadn't been able to follow through on her commitment. She explained her actions by saying that it was better to hide the truth from her children rather than cause them to worry.

Each time I witnessed Christians leaving out details or telling little lies, I felt justified in my own dishonesty. Certainly I recognized a bold lie—especially one designed to hurt others or cause division—but in a politically correct world where the rules seemed to change daily, my search to uncover the truth was not easy. Through studying the Bible and other books on the subject of dishonesty, I finally determined that lying for *any* reason whatsoever was sin in God's eyes. This revelation was a real turning point in my Christian walk, but it was also a challenge because I had to learn to communicate truthfully in all circumstances, which, of course, included my marriage to Joe.

~⊚~

Just before we reconciled, Michelle admitted she was wrong to borrow the money to rectify our overdrawn bank account without my knowledge. Even though her admission was several years after the incident occurred, I was relieved to hear her say she considered her behavior sinful based on God's Word. I knew she and her family believed that withholding truth for the sake of avoiding conflict was a normal and acceptable practice. So each time Michelle became defensive about her lying, I wondered how many other times she had been deceitful with me.

A couple of years after we reconciled and started serving in ministry together, we realized that many couples whose marriages were in crisis struggled in the area of dishonesty the same way we had. One lady who contacted us was worried about how to tell her husband she had spent all the money in their savings account. Their income had dropped and rather than adjust their expenses, she dipped into their savings each month. By the time the truth was disclosed, their marriage was in severe crisis and barely survived.

Dishonesty in marriage creates an emotional wall between a husband and wife. When there is deception in a marriage, it is impossible to be the kind of spouse God calls us to be: "Nevertheless, each individual among you also is to love his own wife even as himself, and the wife must see to it that she respects her husband" (Ephesians 5:33 NASB).

A husband who lies to his wife is saying through his actions, "You don't deserve the truth—I don't love you." And a wife who lies to her husband is saying through her actions, "I don't trust your ability to handle the truth—I don't respect you."

My own struggle with dishonesty was different than Michelle's. I withheld the truth from her when it came to expressing how I really felt about certain things. For example, for the first several years of our marriage—and even after we reconciled—Michelle planned how we would spend our holidays. It didn't bother me that she did the planning, but I resented her for not asking for my input. But instead of letting Michelle know how I felt, I just acted as if it didn't bother me. One Christmas, she could tell I was frustrated, and she had to practically pry the reason out of me. Once I admitted the reason for my frustration, we were able to make a few changes. However, had the reason stayed hidden, I would have remained silently irritated and nothing would have changed. Over the years, I've learned that taking the risk to be real with Michelle creates a deeper level of intimacy between us. The motto we like to live by and tell others to live by is something we once heard from a Christian speaker: "High risk equals high intimacy, and low risk equals low intimacy."

MOTIVES FOR DISHONESTY IN MARRIAGE

In *His Needs, Her Needs,* Willard Harley suggests there are three kinds of lying husbands: the "protector" liar, the "avoid-trouble" liar, and the "born" liar.[1] We have taken the liberty to add a fourth: the "control-freak" liar. Based on what other couples in crisis marriages have told us and from our own experience, one or more of these underlying motives can be found at the root of dishonest behavior—and they don't apply just to men.

1. Lying to protect others. Soon after I (Michelle) vowed to be honest in *all* circumstances, a friend came to me and asked forgiveness for something she had said. I told her that I hadn't even noticed the offense and not to worry about it. After walking away, however, the Holy Spirit convicted me. The truth was that I *had* noticed and I was hurt by what she said. Wanting to protect my friend (and keep her from feeling badly about what she had done), I had obstructed her character growth *and* mine by invalidating her conviction and refusing her apology. It wasn't easy, but the following day I went to her and asked her forgiveness for not being honest.

Protecting others from painful consequences may seem noble at the time, until we realize that God wants to use those very opportunities to discipline and mature us and perhaps do the same for the others involved. Some common examples of missed opportunities for honesty would include lying for a spouse who is too hungover to go to work or covering for someone who is too irresponsible or undisciplined to keep their commitments.

2. Lying to avoid trouble. One of the couples who reconciled their marriage and now serves with us in ministry admits that dishonesty was the biggest problem in their marriage. Joyce hid things from John constantly in order to avoid trouble. She recalls how this affected almost every aspect of their life until she finally repented: "I could never let John answer the phone because it might be a bill collector calling. Since he didn't even know we had money problems, I had to be home when he was in order to answer the phone. It also meant that each time the phone rang I had to race to answer it. The only time I could relax was on Saturday and Sunday because the bill collectors didn't call on weekends.

"Once I finally confessed to John that we were in debt, the relief was so much better than all the stress I felt trying to stay out of trouble and keep him from finding out. And he wasn't even as mad as I thought he would be. The guilt I felt as a result of lying to John had driven a wedge between us, and telling him the truth created a close-ness that had been lacking for a long time."

3. Lying for no apparent reason. A "born" liar lies just for the sake of lying. Willard Harley believes this behavior begins at childhood and is so ingrained, the chances of changing are almost impossible. These lies are not well thought out, making the untruth easier to discover. We've noticed that people who are chronic liars tend to exaggerate details of events to the point of absurdity. Oftentimes they will include their spouse or other family members into a conversation just to vali-date their stories.

One lady shared that she has trouble believing anything her hus-band says and sees his behavior as a character flaw that needs to change in order to save their marriage: "My husband likes to be the center of attention at parties and large gatherings. He constantly exaggerates experiences in order to entertain people or make them laugh. Because I'm standing right there, everyone assumes what he's saying is true. When I try to confront him afterward, he just laughs and tells me I'm making a big deal out of nothing or that he simply forgot the exact details." While this husband may be laughing, his wife has lost respect for him and their marriage is in crisis—and he doesn't even realize it!

Since chronic lying begins early in life, we always tell parents to confront and deal with dishonesty as soon as they see it in their chil-dren. Letting a child get away with lying about something as trivial as who ate the last cookie could actually be setting that child up for chronic lying in adulthood.

4. Lying to control people or circumstances. In our own marriage, as well as others who have come through our ministry, controlling the outcome of a situation tends to be a big motive for dishonesty. Many people whose marriages are in crisis admit they or their spouse have manipulated details, left out facts, or just plain lied in order to make certain things turn out the way they wanted.

When Bea's husband told her he was going to call a relative in another state to check out the prospect of a job transfer, she decided to make sure a job wasn't available so they wouldn't have to move. "I know it was wrong, but at the time I was so freaked out about leaving the life I'd grown accustomed to and moving away from my grown children that I wanted to stop the move at any cost. So I called a relative in the state that my husband wanted to move to and pleaded with her to say there were no job openings when he contacted her." Bea's motive for lying to her husband—and asking someone else to lie as well—was about controlling the outcome of her circumstances, rather than trusting her husband to make the right decision.

Modeling Dishonesty in the Home

Maybe you've seen this commercial: A mom races into a store and buys a new teddy bear for her daughter. She hurries back home and proceeds to cover the bear with mud, washes it several times, and finally runs it over with her car. Then, she puts the teddy bear in the back seat of the car and picks up her young daughter from school. When the little girl gets into the car and sees the teddy bear, she squeals, "Oh! You've found Teddy!" Her mother nods and smiles knowingly at us—the viewers—as if to say, "Any good mom would have done the same thing." Whatever else the advertiser of that commercial was selling, the message that comes across loud and clear is that dishonest behavior in certain circumstances is not only acceptable, but clever and admirable!

Are all your actions and motives aligned with the truth? Begging your spouse to stop lying or disciplining your child for being dishonest won't help either of them change their behavior if you aren't modeling honesty yourself. Ask the Lord to reveal any and all of the ways in which you are modeling dishonest behavior. Then, be ready and willing to hear His answers. Here are a few common examples of modeling dishonest behavior:

- Lying to your spouse or children for any reason (most children know when a parent is lying).
- Giving a false address so your child can attend the "right" school.
- Writing a note so your child will not get a lower grade due to an unexcused absence or a missed homework assignment.
- Instructing your spouse or child to tell an unwanted caller that you aren't home when you actually are.
- Protecting your child against a deserved punishment or consequence from the other parent by lying or covering for them.
- Fibbing about a child's age in order to get cheaper rates at restaurants, movies, amusement parks, etc.
- Telling your family how upset you are with someone, yet not being honest with the person with whom you have the issue.
- Calling in sick to work when you aren't.
- Changing price tags on an item you can't afford.
- Giving someone a false reason for not attending a meeting, party, church service, or other get-together.
- Lying to bill collectors or authorities to protect yourself or someone else from consequences.

Living in the Light

If there is one thing that will sabotage a marriage—or any relationship for that matter—it is dishonesty. Deception is Satan's tool to divide and conquer marriages, families, and the church. "He [the devil] was a murderer from the beginning, not holding to the truth, for there is no truth in him. When he lies, he speaks his native language, for he is a liar and the father of lies" (John 8:44).

One way Satan deceives people is by convincing them to hide their struggles, self-destructive thoughts, addictions, or negative emotions. God wants us to bring everything to the light and walk in freedom: "If you hold to my teaching, you are really my disciples. Then you will know the truth, and the truth will set you free" (John 8:31-32).

Are you holding back from telling the truth and living in darkness in any area of your life? If so, the intimacy in your marriage is blocked, and it will be impossible for your marriage to glorify God. Deception was the root cause as to why my (Michelle) marriage to my first husband, John, ended in divorce.

As a child, I loved reading romance fairytales and believed that finding the right "prince" and having a dream wedding would guarantee my happiness. Unfortunately, when I married in 1965, I didn't have a dream wedding.

I married my high school boyfriend at the age of 17 and lied when I told him he was the father of the child I was carrying. When Elicia was born, John was in Vietnam. I thought about telling him the truth when he returned from the war, but decided against it. As a result, there was an emotional wall between us that continued to grow, even after giving birth to our own daughter, M'Lissa, two years later. Instead of being honest with John and working on the issues in our marriage, I falsely believed it was best to keep the truth buried. When he said he wanted a trial separation so he could "sow some wild oats," I responded by filing for a divorce.

I started dating immediately and remarried as soon as my divorce from John was final in 1970. When Heather was born (within the first year), my new marriage was already in crisis. Ken said he loved me, but wasn't sure if he wanted to stay married. His lack of commitment, combined with my insecurities, led to our separation soon after Heather's birth. During this time, my first husband, John, had repented of his "oat-sowing" and wanted to reconcile. Not wanting to be alone, I remarried him when my divorce from Ken was final.

It was soon after John's and my remarriage in 1973 that I attended the weeklong Christian crusade and was baptized. When John and I relocated to Alaska a couple of weeks later, I never got involved in a church. Sadly, I continued to hide the truth about my first pregnancy, and shortly after our remarriage many of the same problems John and I had the first time around haunted us once again. We divorced for the second time, just two years later in 1975.

I didn't realize the loneliness in my heart could have been filled with Jesus' love. Instead, I turned away from God's love and sought out man's love, marrying again within two years. This time the results were even more damaging. The man I married was controlling and abusive in many ways. Although I didn't attend a church, I began to pray and read the Bible alone in the evenings, searching for answers that would help me make lasting changes in my life.

One of the initial changes I made was to finally disclose the truth about my first pregnancy. Elicia was almost a teenager by then, and I was able to locate her biological father, Steve, living in the state of Washington. When I called and told Steve the truth, his reply was a welcome relief: "Michelle, I always knew Elicia was my daughter. You have just restored my faith in women." He said he was happy to finally have her in his life again. Steve and Elicia connected by writing letters until they were able to meet face-to-face a year later.

I believe God blessed my desire to be honest about Elicia's biological father, because everyone in our families—including Steve's extended family members and my other two daughters and their fathers—accepted the truth amazingly well. There has never been a moment that I regretted telling everyone the truth. In fact, Elicia recently turned 40 and the whole family threw a surprise birthday party for her. When it was time for the guests to go up to the microphone and give Elicia a birthday blessing, Steve (her biological father) was one of the first people to come forward. With tears in his eyes he said, "Elicia, you are so special to me and I'm grateful you have given me four precious grandchildren—they are the highlight of my life!"

As Steve spoke, I couldn't help thinking about how different Elicia's and Steve's lives would have been had I not come forward with the truth. Not only would Elicia have been robbed of knowing her biological father, grandfather, and other family members, but Steve would have missed being a grandparent to Elicia and Joey's four children. Prior to disclosing the truth, Satan had convinced me that being honest about my pregnancy would only cause everyone involved pain and heartache. Instead, the opposite proved to be true. Hiding the truth destroyed two marriages and created guilt that hovered over me like a dark cloud waiting to dampen any chance of living a life worthy of happiness. Exposing the lie lifted the cloud, and God was able to take what Satan meant as harm and transform it into many blessings, including the ones that would be carried on into my relationship with Joe.

Elicia's fortieth birthday party was celebrated with everyone who loved her. And I felt blessed to see how far Joe and I had come over the years as he warmly embraced the attendance of both Elicia's biological father, Steve, and my first husband, John.

~§~

I (Joe) always admired Michelle for telling the truth about her first pregnancy. It was the right thing to do, and God blessed the outcome. When Michelle and I look back over the years at how far our family has come, we know God's hand is in it. Satan wanted to destroy our family—and he almost did—but God took everything and turned it to good, as Romans 8:28 promises: "And we know that in all things God works for the good of those who love him, who have been called according to his purpose."

Having said that, we must also remember that even though God works things out for those who love Him, there are consequences we still have to live with. Guys ask me all the time how I handle being around Michelle's ex-husbands. I admit to them that in the beginning of our marriage, dealing with this was a real struggle. Now I view things differently. God created the girls' dads just as He created me, so how can I show disrespect to God by disrespecting the people He created? Steve (Elicia's dad), John (M'Lissa's dad), and Ken (Heather's dad) will always be their biological fathers—I can't change that. They gave the girls away at their weddings, and they will be included in all the special occasions for their daughters. That's the reality. When I became a Christian, I made the decision that the best way to love my stepdaughters was to show respect to their biological fathers. In the past it was difficult, but with God's help and the Holy Spirit inside me, I am now able to love others as Christ loves me.

Truth with Consequences

As Joe said, there are consequences to our behavior that we will always have to live with. Even so, when we obey God and do what's right, He can use those consequences for His glory. I'll never forget the way I learned this lesson through the eyes of our son, Mick.

When Mick was six years old, while Joe and I were still separated, he began making comments about visiting his dad like his sisters visited theirs. Mick had questions concerning the girls' dads, and I knew that eventually he would find out the truth about my past marriages and divorces. I decided to tell him the truth myself by giving Mick a simple testimony of my life. (At this point I could honestly say it had changed, even though Joe and I had not yet reconciled.)

"Mick, would you like to hear the story of my life?" I asked him one day. With wide eyes and an excitement in his voice he said, "Yeah!" Using photo albums, I explained to him as simply as I could, the events leading up to his dad and I meeting, marrying, and his own birth. I also explained the choices and consequences of not following God and living by His Word. The conversation ended by telling Mick that even though his dad and I were now both Christians, there were still consequences that we had to learn to work through because of our pasts.

The next day after I picked Mick up at school, he asked, "Mom, when we get home, would you tell me the story of your life again?"

"No, son, we don't need to keep talking about it," I answered, wondering what the effects would be of having been that honest with a six-year-old.

As the years passed, Mick didn't ask to hear the story of my life again until one day when he was almost 13. At the time, he was attending a youth group at our church and Jenny, one of the girls in the group, needed a ride for several weeks. One night after the meeting, when I arrived to pick them up from church, Mick walked to the car while Jenny hung back with her arms folded, looking at the ground.

"Mom," Mick began, "Jenny thinks she's done so many bad things in her life that Jesus will never be able to forgive her. Would you tell her the story of your life?" While driving Jenny home, I gave her the condensed version of my life story—and helped her to find the forgiveness, grace, and love of Jesus Christ as her Savior.

It would be so wonderful if my testimony was one that included being able to tell Mick that his dad was my first love, or I'd never told lies that resulted in divorce, and that most of my adult years had been spent serving the Lord. But that will never be. Still, God used the shame of my past to help a young teenage girl find forgiveness and eternal life. Living in the light isn't always easy or comfortable, but if we want God to work out the consequences of past sins for His glory, we cannot allow our sins to hide in the dark.

Five Questions to Help You Choose Truth

We have learned over the years that the best way to avoid falling back into our old, dishonest behavior is to watch for "red-flag" warnings. We use five questions to help us choose truth rather than hide issues in the dark. Try asking yourself these questions the next time you are tempted to tell your spouse or others a little white lie.

1. Am I trying to "play God" in this situation? In Genesis 27 we read about Rebekah, who helped her younger son deceitfully take the blessing and birthright away from his older brother. Rebekah's actions didn't keep God from working out His will, but her deception resulted in never being able to see her favored son again. If we use dishonest means to help others get what they want or think they need, we will never know the full blessings of God in that particular situation because He cannot bless sin and disobedience. God's will always prevails, but if we want His blessings, we must walk in truth.

2. Is my dishonest behavior getting in the way of a valuable lesson from God? Most of us would agree some of the best lessons in life have come from our mistakes and failures. Paul writes, "Endure hardship as discipline; God is treating you as sons" (Hebrews 12:7). Yet it is so tempting to be manipulative or lie in order to "help" others or ourselves avoid the painful consequences of sin.

3. Do I fear the reaction of people instead of fearing (or revering) God? Because there were so many times in our marriage that we hid things to avoid conflict, this question helps us keep our focus on God rather than each other. The Bible is filled with examples of people who lied to the religious rulers of the day because they feared the reaction of others rather than God. "Yet at the same time many even among the leaders believed in Him. But because of the Pharisees they would not confess their faith for fear they would be put out of the synagogue; for they loved praise from men more than praise from God" (John 12:42-43).

4. Who am I when no one else is looking? When no one else is around and your actions may be hidden from others, God still sees you, and you still have to look at yourself in the mirror at the end of the day. Our coleaders in ministry, Mark and Debbie, often share this example from their own marriage: Mark had suspected that Debbie had fallen back into some old patterns of behavior. When Mark finally took the risk to confront Debbie, she lied. "I knew there was no way Mark could prove his accusations, and I wasn't about to admit I'd made such a stupid mistake after all those years. I held my ground and thought I'd convinced him his suspicions were imagined. When the discussion was over, I breathed a sigh of relief and walked into the bathroom to get ready for work. Then, I looked at myself in the mirror. I may have fooled Mark, but one look in the mirror reminded me I hadn't fooled God, and I was nothing but a liar. After repenting to the Lord for lying to my husband, I went to Mark to ask his forgiveness and come clean. His response was so Christlike that I've never forgotten it. He lovingly said, 'Debbie, I knew you lied to me, but I trusted you to eventually do what was right and tell the truth.'"

5. Is the situation I'm facing right now a result of a previous deception? In Debbie's case her initial deception led to her dilemma of whether or not to tell Mark the truth when he finally confronted her. If she had not been receptive to the Holy Spirit's conviction when she looked at herself in the mirror, she would have added yet another layer of deceit to her circumstances. If there has been a pattern of layering lies to cover other lies, consequences will become more complex.

Telling the Truth—God's Way

At some point, if true healing and honesty are to occur, it will be necessary to peel back those layers one at a time. That's what happened in Lynne's case. When Lynne made a decision to accept Christ as her

Savior, the first change she made in her life was to break off a three-year affair and commit to working on her troubled marriage. Several months later her husband, Steve, made a commitment to Christ, and the two of them decided to get marriage counseling from their pastor. As he normally did, the pastor asked to meet with each one privately once or twice before seeing them as a couple. During Lynne's private counseling session, she admitted to her pastor she had broken off the affair, but had not yet confessed the affair to Steve.

"One day you will have to tell Steve, and God will let you know when," the pastor told her. The idea of telling Steve terrified her so much she made a decision to keep her secret buried, regardless of her pastor's prediction. As time went on, the pastor's words kept ringing in Lynne's ears. She would have to tell Steve one day, and God would let her know when. A couple of years later, God opened the door that Lynne had been dreading. When she stepped through that door in obedience and told Steve the truth, she received a blessing from God. Although Steve was hurt, he forgave her and they were able to work through the crisis with their pastor. They stayed married and now serve in full-time ministry together.

If you have been hiding a secret from your spouse that God wants brought to the light, He will provide the opportunity, even if you have plans to keep your secret buried. Your part will be to obey God and trust Him with the outcome.

❧

During our second separation, and before rededicating my (Michelle) life to Christ, I spent a weekend with someone from my past. I decided never to tell Joe about the incident. However, six years later while I was reading a book on marriage, God let me know He had other plans. The author of the book wrote that he didn't think it was necessary for an unfaithful spouse to admit their affair. When I read those words, instead of feeling relieved that hiding my weekend affair was okay according to this Christian author, the opposite occurred: I was convicted. I tried to push the conviction far from my mind. For days I wrestled and argued with the Lord and frantically searched His Word for a way out of having to confess a weekend affair. *After all, I reasoned, that affair took place six years ago, well before either of us was following the Lord.*

Finally, recognizing all the signs of deceitful scheming, I told Joe that there was something I had to confess. The fear was overwhelming, because we were now serving in ministry and helping other couples to reconcile. I knew if our marriage blew apart, other relationships would suffer as well. Shaking, I told Joe what I had done. The first look on his face was shock, followed by anger. Then my worst fear occurred—Joe left.

Would he come back? Would he fall into his old patterns of behavior and go to a bar? Would he be able to forgive me for all the years I had hidden the affair? What would I tell the kids and everyone at church if we separated again?...

The questions were endless and all I could do was cry, wait, and continue to tell God that I trusted Him to honor my obedience.

An hour later, Joe walked back through the door. He hadn't been drinking. He was still visibly angry, but seemed much calmer. He sat in a chair in the living room and avoided eye contact with me. I decided rather than to force a conversation, I'd just quietly slip off to bed and let God continue to work. The next morning, Joe finally spoke: "Michelle, is there anything else you have kept hidden from me over the years? Because if there is, you'd better tell me now. I don't ever want another bombshell like the one you dropped on me last night."

I told Joe the truth, assuring him that there weren't any more secrets. What he did next was an unexpected surprise, and it was God's gift to me for fearing Him rather than Joe. Joe took me in his arms, and thanked me for telling him the truth.

Because I had no one else to depend on except God and no guarantees as to how Joe would respond, this step of faith resulted in deepening my walk with the Lord. After that experience, I trusted God's leading more than ever.

～◎～

That situation was a turning point for me (Joe) as well. I realized that Michelle's only motive for telling me the truth was to please God. She had gotten away with the deception for six years, and the chance of my ever discovering the truth was slim to none. Once I realized her fear of God was as strong as it was, it gave me a new sense of peace in our relationship.

Are Little White Lies Ever Acceptable?

Taking off all falsehood for the sake of having a better marriage and not letting the sun go down on your anger should be great incentives for avoiding dishonesty. But the number one reason for being honest in all circumstances should be to honor God. We are His vessels, and the Holy Spirit lives in us. How can you be a representative and a witness for the Lord if there is deception in your life? In all our years of ministry and helping couples in crisis, we have never known a single instance where a person has rejoiced over discovering that his or her spouse told little white lies to avoid conflict, protect him- or herself, or control circumstances. If you believe you have to lie to your spouse in order to have a good marriage, you have believed a lie yourself. God would never look favorably on a husband and wife lying to one another. "For the LORD your God detests anyone who does these things, anyone who deals dishonestly" (Deuteronomy 25:16).

The Delicate Dance of Tasteful Transparency

At this point, you might be asking, *Do you expect me to tell my spouse everything? And just how honest am I supposed to be with everyone?* We aren't recommending that you rush out and unload everything you've hidden from your spouse over the years, or that you start telling your friends and family everything you've ever felt about them. We are suggesting, however, that you take the time to let the Holy Spirit bring to light anything He wants you to reveal in your life, then be ready to listen and follow the process God places before you. God wants you to be a person of truth, integrity, clarity, and honesty in every area of your life. But He also desires balance in everything you do: "Accurate weights are his delight" (Proverbs 11:1).

Here are four ways to help you keep truth in balance:

1. Proceed with caution and prayer before telling anyone a truth or secret that you wouldn't want others to know or hasn't been previously disclosed. If there is something in your past or a secret sin you are struggling with that needs to come into the light, you will be able to trust only a handful of people with it. These people may include your spouse, your pastor, a licensed counselor, a recovery support group leader, or anyone else who is under obligation to keep what is shared confidential. It would be nice if everyone could be trusted with our secrets, but the truth is, people are human and confidences are broken.

At a retreat I attended once, it came time for the women to share how the weekend had blessed them, and a lady tearfully admitted that her husband had just revealed to her that he'd been having an affair. Sharing her burden with the women wasn't necessarily the problem, but what she did next pushed her sharing out of balance. She told everyone that the couple's teenage children had not yet been informed about their father's affair and asked all 120 women in that room to please keep what she had just shared confidential. Her request put an unfair burden on the women in the room, not to mention putting her marriage and children's best interests at risk. Always tell the truth, but proceed through the entire process with caution and choose with whom to share certain truths wisely and carefully.

2. *Ask permission before sharing someone else's truth—especially your spouse's.* If your spouse has taken a risk to be vulnerable with you by confessing a secret sin or struggle and you share it with others without his or her permission, you will cause damage in your marriage and harm your chances of ever being trusted again. Even if your spouse isn't willing to keep what you share confidential, make it your prayer to honor what is shared between the two of you. As you model your allegiance to your spouse in this area, you will gain his/her respect and trust and create a safe place for your spouse to be real with you. This will also increase your chances of being treated the same way.

Always get permission *before* sharing anything that people tell you about their pasts or a struggle they are facing in the present—even if you are sharing it as a prayer request. Satan would like nothing better than to have prayer used to spread gossip or break confidences and divide Christians.

3. *Ask God to examine your motives.* The desire for power or control has an uncanny way of being disguised behind a smoke screen of love and concern. Honest motives must always precede telling the truth. Bringing something into the light about others—including your spouse—should be bathed in prayer first. If you have information about someone that you think needs to be disclosed, ask God to help you examine and understand your motives first. You may be telling the truth, but if your motive is for any purpose other than honoring the Lord, it is the same as dishonest behavior.

4. Make sure the truth you are about to share is necessary to disclose.
Telling your spouse you had to repent to the Lord for looking twice
at an attractive person while shopping might be true, but it may not
be necessary. Even if you honestly wish your spouse would get laser
treatment for aging skin, a new hair color, tooth-whitening, or an new
style of clothing, telling him or her just might do more harm than
good. Also, describing every detail of an affair, just so you can be completely honest (especially if your spouse hasn't asked) might be more
information than is necessary and could actually hinder the healing
process. Before disclosing anything, be sure to also ask God about the
way in which the information should be disclosed. Good communication skills, word choice, listening skills, and body language are of the
utmost importance.

Another factor to consider is that some spouses can handle more
truth and detail than others. The only way you will know how much
yours can handle is to go to the Lord in prayer before going to your
spouse. If you are so honest with your spouse that you continually
hurt his or her feelings or show disrespect, then perhaps your motives
for telling the truth are self-seeking and out of balance. If you truly
want to honor God with your honesty, He will help you determine if
the truth and the details you are about to disclose are necessary.

To Tell or Not to Tell

There is never a reason to lie to your spouse. But disclosing something from your past, especially if it's something you did before you
met, is a separate issue. If you have a secret sin from your past and
wonder if or when you should tell your spouse, there's only one way
to know for sure: Ask God to reveal the answer. There's no simple
formula to follow, but based on experiences of couples we have coun-
seled over the years and from our own experience, here are a few
questions to consider:

- Has your spouse ever asked you point-blank about the particular sin from your past and you have yet to disclose the truth? For example, having an abortion, spending time in jail, substance abuse, a previous marriage, an affair, etc.
- Have you ever been told by a pastor, health-care professional, or licensed counselor that you should disclose the sin from your past to your spouse?
- Has the Holy Spirit ever stirred your heart in such a way that you know you should disclose the truth, but instead you delayed your obedience?
- Are you struggling with obsessive thoughts or guilt about the sin from your past?
- Are thoughts from your past affecting your sleeping or eating habits?
- Has sin from your past affected your ability to have satisfying sex or deep levels of intimacy with your spouse?
- Can you discuss your past with friends or relatives but feel you have to hide it from your spouse?

If you answered yes to any of these questions, it would probably be a good idea to consider talking to your spouse about the secret(s) you are hiding. Your spouse has the right know you better than anyone else. If you answered no to the questions, continue to pray and ask God to reveal His answer in His time. Then let your past rest in the forgiving arms of the Lord.

◦⊙◦

If you are thinking right now that you have to keep your secrets in the dark because your marriage isn't strong enough to survive a painful confession or disclosure from your past, you are wrong. If your marriage is in crisis, being totally honest with your spouse is the only way your marriage will have hope of surviving. Even if your spouse refuses to take the risk to be open and honest, you can still do your part.

GROUP OR SUPPORT-PARTNER DISCUSSION QUESTIONS

1. *Based on the motives for dishonesty on pages 112-115, discuss the reasons people are dishonest.*
2. *Discuss the five questions on pages 122-123 that can help you choose truth.*
3. *Do you think it's possible to be "too honest"? Discuss how to have balance.*
4. *Have you had an opportunity to practice any of the tools or exercises in the previous chapter this week? If so, which ones?*
5. *Look up and discuss Proverbs 4:23-27.*
6. *Share at least one thing you are thankful for.*
7. *Share a prayer request.*

8

You Can Develop Healthy Boundaries

For God did not give us a spirit of timidity, but a spirit of power, of love and of self-discipline.

—2 TIMOTHY 1:7

*G*od's perfect will for you and your spouse is to love one another and have a joy-filled marriage that glorifies Him. God hates divorce (Malachi 2:16). However, it's a misconception to think that separation should never be an option. Over the years, we've seen many cases where separation was the wake-up call that an unrepentant spouse needed to break off an affair or receive help for abusive or addictive behavior. And, as with us, many couples, together or individually, have become Christians or rededicated their lives to Christ during a painful separation.

We regularly receive calls from people in abusive or adulterous marriages. Many of them admit they fear putting healthy boundaries in place because doing so might result in separation. We realize the issue of separation can be controversial among Christians, and we do not take this subject lightly. We will never be advocates of divorce, but we disagree with the belief that separation under *any* circumstance is wrong. As long as reconciliation is the goal, we believe separation—especially in the case of abuse or unrepentant adultery—is acceptable for Christians. "A wife must not separate from her husband. But if she does, she must remain unmarried or else be reconciled to her husband" (1 Corinthians 7:10-11).

A man or woman whose spouse is physically abusive, continues to commit adultery, or sexually abuses his or her children should be held accountable for these actions. To allow a spouse to continue with this kind of destructive and sinful behavior is to disrespect the high regard that God has placed on marriage and family. When a husband or wife is afraid to set healthy boundaries in these situations, we call this a "fear-based marriage." A marriage commitment based on the fear of man is not honoring to the Lord. Fear of God is different than fear of man. Fearing God means you have a holy reverence for Him and for His Word. God tells us throughout His Word we are to fear Him, not each other. "Fear of man will prove to be a snare, but whoever trusts in the LORD is kept safe" (Proverbs 29:25).

FEAR: THE INVISIBLE FIRE

If you've ever had a problem with rust on outdoor furniture or a car, you know if the rust isn't removed, it will eventually destroy the metal. The reason rust is so damaging is because its corrosive power is like an invisible, slow-moving fire that burns its way through the metal. That's exactly what happens when your marriage is fear-based. The emotion of fear is invisible, but it is strong enough to destroy love. If you just "paint" over the problems in your marriage with kind words or pretense, you won't ever remove the fear, and "rust" will continue to destroy your marriage.

Many people we minister to are focused only on the symptoms of their marital problems instead of getting to the root of the dissension. People complain about how their spouses cheat, drink, rage, or have addictions, rather than taking responsibility for setting boundaries that can produce repentance and change. In these situations, a physical separation can create the time and space needed for a spouse who is falling to pieces emotionally to set healthy boundaries. With the help of their support system (based on the tools in chapter 2), a husband or wife can stand back and gain a clearer perspective of their crisis marriage because they aren't living amid the chaos of an abusive relationship.

The problem is that due to the controversy surrounding separation, most people—especially Christians—wait too long before taking a stand against the unacceptable behavior of their spouses. As a result, many of the separations that happen by the time healthy boundaries are in place end up being transitions to divorce. We have seen many repentant spouses served with divorce papers by an emotionally exhausted mate who had nothing left to work on the marriage. That's what happened in Natalie's case.

A couple of years into her marriage to Larry, Natalie became restless and bored. One of the ways she found to break the boredom was to party with her girlfriends. When Larry begged her to stop and said he wanted to start a family, Natalie refused his request. Larry believed the best thing he could do to keep their marriage from unraveling was to give her some space. He avoided giving Natalie an ultimatum or setting boundaries, because he was afraid she would leave. Eventually Natalie met someone and later admitted to Larry that she had been unfaithful. Her affair was the last straw. When Larry finally got up the courage to give Natalie an ultimatum of choosing between their marriage and her sinful lifestyle, his worst fear was confirmed. Natalie moved out.

Several months later, Natalie called our ministry in tears. "I have been such a fool! I took advantage of a wonderful man who really loved me. I want Larry back, and I'm willing to do anything to save our marriage. But the problem is, my husband has found someone else and says God brought this woman into his life!"

I (Michelle) spoke with Natalie several times and encouraged her to focus on God and wait patiently for her husband to come to his senses. Over the next several months she attended classes, joined a support group, and was truly repentant of her past behaviors. She and their pastor tried everything to convince Larry to break off his relationship with the other woman and to work on reconciling their marriage. He never did. Larry filed for divorce, and the week it was finalized he married the woman "God gave him."

Larry and Natalie's separation was the wake-up call that God used to get Natalie's attention and turn her life back to Him. But when Natalie repented, Larry was long gone. In his emotionally and spiritually worn-out condition, he bought into the lie that God had someone else waiting for him.

Putting healthy boundaries in place may result in separation or divorce, but not doing so may also result in divorce. Many Christian counselors agree. In their book *Boundaries in Marriage,* psychologists Henry Cloud and John Townsend write: "In one sense, people with real boundaries could avoid many divorces. But they might have to take a strong stance; separate, not participate in the behavioral patterns against which they are setting boundaries; and demand righteousness before participating in the relationship again. If they become the light, then the other person either changes or goes away. This is why, in most cases, we say you really should not have to be the one who divorces."[1]

Dr. James Dobson also agrees. In his book *Love Must Be Tough,* he warns that spouses who don't put boundaries in place lose the respect of the adulterous spouse and the marriage has less chance of surviving.[2]

We believe many Christian couples appear happy on the outside, but on the inside one spouse is silently suffering because he or she has a fear-based marriage and needs to set healthy boundaries, but for one reason or another is reluctant to do so. Obviously, we aren't saying you must separate in order to save your crisis marriage. In fact, sometimes God works in miraculous ways that confound our common sense. We know one man who patiently waited two years for his wife to end her affair—and she finally did. And we know that there are Christians who say that even if a spouse is physically abusive, God will protect the innocent victim and that neither the abuser nor the victim should leave the home. One pastor claims he stopped physically abusing his wife because she loved him through it and didn't leave.

While we know that all things are possible with God, these two examples are not the norm. In most cases, a person who doesn't suffer the natural consequences of his or her actions will not recognize their need for change. While separation should be the last option, it is often necessary when unrepentant, illegal, or immoral behavior takes place in the home.

Set Boundaries with a Soft Heart

If you set boundaries when your heart is hard and vindictive, you can actually make things worse. A soft heart doesn't mean being passive. Jesus turned over the money changers' tables and confronted the religious leaders of His day with a soft heart. Even if your anger is justified, it doesn't warrant retaliation in God's eyes. Except in cases of physical abuse or child endangerment, wait to put boundaries in place until you can do so with a soft heart. A person with a soft heart is one who is willing to look at his or her own sin before helping others with theirs. The first step in setting boundaries with a soft heart is to identify areas in your marriage that are fear-based and then take responsibility for your part.

Here are the most common reasons we have witnessed, as well as experienced, as to why people keep the peace until they fall to pieces.

As you read through these reasons, ask God to reveal His truth and wisdom to your heart. Sometimes you may think you are the offended person in your marriage or maybe even a victim until God gives you wisdom from His perspective.

1. Fear of rejection. Some people have admitted they tolerate the abuse or adultery on the part of their spouse because they just don't want to end up alone. In their book *Safe People,* Cloud and Townsend call this "the fear of abandonment" and cite it as being one of the main reasons people don't implement healthy boundaries:

> Many times someone who is in a painful relationship should set
> strong disciplinary boundaries or cut off the relationship for a
> time. But he [or she] fears being alone so much that he can't do
> it. Every time the person thinks of standing up to the other per-
> son, or getting out of the relationship, he [or she] is overwhelmed
> by feelings of loss and aloneness, and either avoids taking the dif-
> ficult step to begin with, or quickly caves in.[3]

God created us with two needs: Him and other people. Before you implement healthy boundaries in your marriage, make sure your support system is in place. Then, trust God to supply your needs through His presence in your heart as well as the people He places in your path.

2. Emotionally immature responses. Many people admit they try to keep the peace at all costs because they or their spouses are not able to handle confrontation or conflict. If you have an emotional meltdown every time things don't go your way, you will cause your spouse to walk on eggshells in order to avoid setting you off. And if you are the one walking on eggshells, your unhealthy communication skills will not help your spouse mature. This learned negative behavior can be unlearned more quickly than you think. Sometimes just realizing the toll emotionally immature behavior puts on other members of the family can be enough to change bad habits. One lady who has been happily married for 35 years shared: "While growing up, I used to overreact to everything. My parents and siblings just accepted it. But the first time my husband saw one of these childish outbursts, his reaction to my behavior caused me to see how immature I was. His eyes grew wide and he said, 'Why, I don't think I've ever seen a grown woman act quite like that before!' My husband wasn't being mean, he was just being very matter-of-fact. I felt so embarrassed about my behavior, that I decided right then and there he would never see me act like that again. And he hasn't."

A woman who sobs uncontrollably or a husband who stomps and sulks might get what he or she wants the first few times but eventually it will breed disrespect and meaningful communication will shut down. We've spoken to many people who live with an emotionally immature spouse, but most of them admit they feel more like a parent than a partner.

If your spouse is emotionally immature, the worst thing you can do is give in to his or her demands. That kind of response will only perpetuate the problem. Communicate honestly and tell your spouse you disapprove of his or her childish behavior in the home—and, of course, don't forget to model proper behavior yourself. If your family or friends have told you that you behave childishly, you probably do. Begin now to make changes.

3. Fear of retaliation. Some people are afraid to set boundaries because their spouse plays the "get-even" game. If you or your spouse is keeping score of offenses toward one another, the communication level of your marriage is severely suffering. Recently a woman told me (Michelle) that she feared confronting her husband about his sinful lifestyle, so she just stayed out of his way as much as possible. "When I say things that he doesn't like to hear, I have to pay for it in other ways. He brings up past arguments and all the mistakes I've made. He never lets me forget a thing. It's just not worth trying to communicate, and I'm sure not going to risk telling him that he has to change his behavior either."

Another woman shared that she and her husband call each other names when they argue. Her excuse for participating in the name-calling indicated a desire to even up the score and retaliate: "Why should I stop if he isn't willing to do the same? I know it's not right, but if he isn't going to play fair, I'm not going to either!"

⌒☙⌒

Many of the men I (Joe) talk to complain their wives shut them out emotionally and/or sexually if they make them angry. One man said, "My wife and I will be having a conversation, and then I'll say something that doesn't sit well with her, and she blows up. Instead of talking it out, she sleeps in the guest bedroom for a few days. We don't have kids so we can go several days without communicating or sleeping together in the home. After a while I finally decide it isn't worth it and apologize (even though I'm not exactly sure what I'm apologizing for). Then we make up." This man went on to say he is not happy in his marriage because he fears his wife's revenge or rejection every time he accidentally offends her.

Mistakenly buying into the concept of "fairness" in a marriage indicates that the marriage is some sort of competition, and that concept only perpetuates unhealthy score-keeping. If you tend to keep score of your spouse's offenses and then retaliate, admit your self-centered thinking to God and ask Him to help you see the positive qualities in your spouse. Let go of your unrealistic expectations and get into the habit of giving your disappointments to God each time your spouse lets you down.

4. Fear of being financially destitute. Many people we've met during our years in marriage ministry have expressed they are reluctant to set healthy boundaries because they fear financial destitution. In Bernice's case, her husband's constant threats controlled their interactions and communication during the two years they were married. One motivating factor in Bernice's desire to keep the peace at all costs was her husband's continual reminder that he held the purse strings. "Finally, one day it was like a light bulb went off," she told me (Michelle). "I realized that even if my kids and I lived in our car, it was better than being emotionally abused and stalked every time I went somewhere."

After two years of keeping the peace, Bernice finally called her husband's bluff. She faced her fear of being financially destitute and moved in with a family member for a couple of months. Now she has a job and her own place. In Bernice's case, her move jolted her husband into realizing how much his fear of losing her had caused him to be overly controlling and emotionally abusive. Now he wants to reconcile and they are currently in counseling.

Almost every community has resources in place to help women—especially mothers—get on their feet financially in order to leave a spouse who is abusive or has some type of addiction. In many cases we have watched women return to school or get in-depth counseling for their own problems because they finally faced their fears. A marriage commitment based on the fear of financial problems is no reason to put yourself or your children at risk. Your church family and other faith-based organizations in your community are there to help, so don't be afraid to ask for assistance.

5. Fear of a spouse's controlling behavior. In her book *When Love Dies: The Process of Marital Dissatisfaction*, Karen Kayser refers to emotional abuse and domineering husbands as the turning point when most women fall out of love.[4] H. Norman Wright agrees: "When men become powerful they also tend to become controlling. Control is disastrous in the working world and in marriage. The macho image is contradictory to the Christian man's calling because it puts *him* rather than God at the center of his universe."[5]

I (Michelle) talk with many women who have fallen out of love with their husbands because of their controlling behavior. One woman recently told me: "I would go somewhere, and if my husband thought I was gone too long, he would get in his car and come looking for me. He controlled all the money and reminded me that if it weren't for him I would be nothing and have nothing. If I tried to stand up to him, he would threaten to divorce me. Financially I couldn't afford to be alone and he knew it, so his threats stopped me from communicating with him honestly." In this woman's case, setting healthy boundaries would help her husband take responsibility for his abusive, controlling behavior. Instead, he continues to mistreat her and she continues to lose respect for him and feels like a prisoner in her own home.

☙

Men aren't the only ones who can exhibit controlling behavior. Husbands tell me (Joe) that they don't like it when their wives act more like their mothers than their partners. To most men, this type of behavior feels controlling. When a spouse acts like a parent, intimacy goes right out the door. That was an area of struggle for Michelle and me, because we both possess strong temperaments. Now we use a little cue that works well when either one of us starts to feel controlled and parented rather than encouraged and supported. We say, "Okay, Mom" or "Okay, Dad." It's a nonthreatening and quick way to set up a healthy boundary.

Fear-based conversation due to a controlling spouse will rob couples of deep emotional attachment and intimacy. The best way to find out if your spouse feels controlled by you is to ask him or her. (Of course, you must ask with a heart that is willing to make changes rather than defend your position, as well as be prepared to hear your spouse's honest answer.)

6. Fear of losing children. The fear of losing a custody battle or having children taken away by an angry spouse can be enough to keep a fearful parent from setting healthy boundaries in the home. Jenny admitted she was staying in her marriage because she didn't want her husband to have unsupervised overnight visits with their young daughter. "I don't want to take the risk of him having a woman over, using pornography, or getting drunk when it's his turn to take her." Jenny's fear-based commitment kept her from setting necessary boundaries concerning her husband's sinful behavior.

Unfortunately, we hear these kinds of excuses quite often. Jenny eventually left her home when her husband refused to give up pornography and other women. At present, Jenny doesn't know if her husband will ever repent and desire to reconcile, but she and her daughter are out of the unhealthy environment and living with her parents while she waits for God's answer.

Another woman confided, "I know our marriage isn't healthy. My husband is abusive and controlling, but at least as long as we live together, I can be there to protect our children. If I leave him, how will I be certain they are safe when they visit him?" This woman's fear is certainly understandable, but wives who try to control the level of a husband's abuse just by being present—as well as having their children view abusive behavior—are really not protecting their children at all.

❧

Men and women alike fear custody battles. I (Joe) hear many men say they will never take the risk of setting healthy boundaries in their marriages because they feel the courts might side with their wives. Several of the guys I have ministered to through the years have, in fact, lost custody of their children to women who were on drugs or sleeping with other men. One thing I always tell them is to not speak badly about their wives, and to be the men God has called them to be. Their children will see the difference when it's their turn to visit, and someday the truth will be evident. In most cases, this has been the result.

Some of the men and women we've met were able to get custody without even going to court. Rather than fighting against their spouses, they said things such as, "I don't want to fight you in court. I will trust you to make the right decisions concerning what is best for our children, and I believe you will protect them when they are in your care." We've known of many spouses—even abusive ones—who dropped their defenses once they realized there wasn't going to be a court battle. It's surprising how many people have told us their decision not to fight in court was the one thing that convinced the unrepentant spouse to do what was best concerning the children.

Having said this, however, we also realize sometimes going to court is the only way to deal with an abusive or vindictive spouse. We recommend you pray and get godly counsel before picking up the phone to call an attorney. We know of several families who lost everything because attorneys became involved, and the court battles destroyed any hope of reconciliation. Once the call is made and the legal ball starts rolling, it is almost impossible to stop it. Last year, a woman called our ministry for advice because she and her husband had decided to reconcile after filing for divorce. It ended up costing her close to one thousand dollars just to file the proper papers to stop it.

Pray for your spouse to do what is right for your children. Avoid going to court unless there is illegal, dangerous, or immoral behavior against you or your children. If you are the one fighting a spouse who wants to share custody, be careful how you fight. You may win the battle but eventually lose the war. In most cases, the bitter spouse who wins custody of the children when they are young ends up spending lonely years once the children grow up and hear the other side of the story.

7. Fear of a spouse's anger. Sinful anger explosions can stop a spouse from doing what's necessary to have a healthy marriage. Even though by nature men are known to be more aggressive than women, anger explosions are not gender exclusive. If you or your spouse expresses anger through rage, you can be sure your marriage is fear-based. No one enjoys being blasted by an angry spouse, and most will do anything to avoid a conversation that might set off an explosion of anger.

In his book *Nine Critical Mistakes Most Couples Make*, Dr. David Hawkins writes: "Another critical mistake is using the sharp tongue in an angry, untamed way. Like fire, it is a killer. It destroys people, relationships, and marriages."[6]

Lisa had a hard time setting boundaries because her spouse's anger controlled all their conversations. She learned early in their marriage to avoid any type of conversation that would set him off—especially in public. "When we were first married, I would simply quit speaking if he was on an anger rampage. I refused to feed his rage, knowing it would eventually die out on its own for lack of fuel." Lisa was committed to the marriage but avoided setting boundaries that might result in a separation. She was keeping the peace, but falling to pieces emotionally and physically. After taking classes to help her set healthy boundaries, Lisa changed. "I realized that not setting boundaries wasn't healthy for me. I felt defeated and dishonest when I was mum. I've learned that speaking truth—even when he is raging—is my responsibility. How he processes the truth is his. In the last few years his outbreaks of rage have lessened and because I speak up now, there is no root of bitterness inside of me and I can pray for my husband with a clean heart."

Sometimes a spouse will shut down communication or be dishonest just to keep his or her mate from becoming frustrated or to control the outcome of a particular circumstance. Joe and I laugh about this now, but one time a year or so after we reconciled we were on vacation in Lake Tahoe, California, and Joe said, "Let's go to the restaurant we went to the last time we were here."

"What restaurant is that?" I asked. I had no idea which restaurant Joe was referring to, since we'd been to Lake Tahoe many times.

"You know," he said. He went on to explain the location and the atmosphere of the restaurant, trying to jog my memory.

"I still don't remember," I shrugged.

At that point I noticed Joe was starting to get frustrated because I couldn't recall the restaurant he was referring to. When he continued to try and make me remember, I finally lied so he wouldn't become even more irritated.

"Of course, I remember now." I just wanted to have a good time and avoid the silly bickering going on between us.

On the way to the restaurant (still trying to remember), I forgot to guard my conversation and innocently asked, "Did I like it?"

"I knew it! I knew it! I knew you were just pretending to remember!" As soon as Joe said those words, we both started to laugh. It was obvious that we had both fallen into our old patterns of fear-based conversation. Joe was getting frustrated, and I was trying to fix the situation by putting on falsehood to help control Joe's emotions. Even though the incident occurred over a trivial matter, it was good that we caught it when we did. We know from experience that trivial, fear-based conversations are how habits are sown, leading to deeper fear-based issues down the road. Now if either of us starts to get frustrated because the other one can't remember something, we bring humor to the situation by asking, "Did I like it?"

If you and your spouse have communication problems because of anger issues, it may take the assistance of a pastor or counselor to help you set some healthy boundaries. It may also take calling the authorities on your spouse if he or she becomes violent, destroys property, or threatens you during an anger episode. This type of boundary is difficult to set, but contacting authorities works in many cases because the raging spouse realizes he or she will have to answer to someone other than you the next time an episode occurs. To tiptoe around the truth or shut down communication because you fear your spouse's anger is not honoring to the Lord or your spouse.

If you are the one raging in anger, review the tools in chapter 6; and if you are still unable to implement healthy changes, reach out for help. If your spouse and children are closing off communication with you because of your anger, you are missing an opportunity to emotionally, physically, and spiritually connect with them.

8. *Fear of a spouse's mental breakdown or suicide.* If your spouse threatens suicide, suffers from mental illness, struggles with depression, or reacts to stressful situations violently and aggressively, you must immediately take action to put healthy boundaries in place—even if your spouse makes threats. You will need to seek professional counseling in order to establish healthy boundaries. While you should keep the marriage commitment you made to your spouse "in sickness and in health," that commitment should never be fear-based. Professional counseling and proper medical care will help you understand your spouse's illness and equip you with the tools to come alongside him or her in a healthy manner. Since depression is sometimes a factor in suicide, admitting it and seeking proper treatment are two of the most important things in suicide prevention. If you don't get help and continue to try to keep the peace in your home by yourself, you will only wear yourself out and perhaps unintentionally put someone's life at stake.

Several years ago a woman tried to hide her husband's mental illness because he was a pastor. She was afraid to bring the illness to the light because she knew once she did, her husband would be removed from the pulpit. Instead of reaching out to others, she privately helped prepare his sermons, coached him from the sidelines, and explained his sometimes aggressive behavior as stress-related. This cover-up went on for several years until his illness progressed to the point where she could no longer hide it. She tried to keep the peace at all costs because she feared what would happen once her husband's illness was discovered.

When I (Michelle) spoke with this woman a few years ago, she admitted that once others knew about her husband's condition, it was actually much easier on the whole family. They no longer lived in secrecy and the friends who rallied around her were able to provide the love and encouragement she wasn't getting on her own. Her husband's condition has gotten progressively worse, and although they live in separate dwellings, she continues to care for him daily.

We once heard an illustration about rocks in a riverbed as an example of how God works. The rocks we see in a river are all shiny and pretty, but as soon as you pick one up and look at the underside, it is slimy and dirty. Once the rock is turned over and the water washes it clean, the beauty that was there all along can be seen. Satan would like nothing more than to keep our problems in the dark, but there is power in bringing everything into the light.

If you or your spouse struggles with depression, thoughts of suicide, or mental illness, it's important to have a safe support system that understands the spiritual as well as the medical aspects of these conditions.

9. *Fear of being physically abused or killed.* God wants you to be committed to your spouse until "death do you part." That doesn't mean, however, that you are to stay in an abusive marriage until your spouse kills you and/or your children. Domestic violence—even among Christians—runs rampant. If there is physical, sexual, emo-

tional, or verbal abuse going on in your home, you must immediately put boundaries in place. In these types of situations, the boundaries will probably involve contacting authorities and getting professional help. Depending on your circumstances, it may be necessary and advisable for you to leave the situation until you are no longer in danger. To place you and your children in a situation that is life-threatening was never God's intent when He created marriage and family.

One woman who tried to justify staying in her abusive marriage said, "He doesn't actually hit me, he just shoves me and says things like, 'Why don't you just go kill yourself!'"

Another lady explained the marks on her arm this way: "It's my fault. I pushed him into scratching me. He really isn't abusive unless I make him mad."

And one woman we know, who believes she is lucky to be alive today, said, "I was afraid to leave my husband because when Nicole Simpson's infamous murder hit the media, my husband told me that he would do the same thing to me if I ever tried to leave. I believed him. I finally left when I decided I'd rather be dead than live with his abuse."

If you have never been in an abusive relationship, you won't be able to identify with these statements. But if you have, you know that abuse takes on many forms, and sometimes it isn't until you are free and look back on the relationship that you realize your fear-based commitment was the only reason you stayed. That's what happened in my (Michelle) abusive marriage in Alaska.

After John and I divorced for the second time I mistakenly believed the new person I started dating a few months later was the "knight in shining armor" for whom I'd been searching. He seemed loving in many ways, but his insecurities and secret struggles were masked, and our relationship was unhealthy from the beginning. His desire to control my decisions, finances, business dealings, and daughters seemed like a form of protection at first. I felt taken care of. After we married and time passed, his controlling behavior started getting worse. A few of my friends noticed this and pointed it out to me, but I ignored their warnings. One day a friend said, "Michelle everything in this house looks like him. I don't see anything that represents your own tastes in decorating anymore." She was right about his subtle domination over every aspect of my life, but I couldn't see it at the time.

When he convinced me to sell everything and move to a small village two hundred miles outside of Anchorage, it seemed like an exciting adventure. But with no telephone, no transportation during the winter, and only a handful of people who even knew where we lived, I began to feel isolated and trapped. "You don't need all those friends around. You have me," he would say when I asked to go to Anchorage to visit with friends. When my unhappiness started to show, he became even more insecure—and more controlling. Some of his problems could have been dealt with through professional counseling, but I realize now his biggest problem was spiritual. Each time I suggested we try going to church, he just laughed.

One day, after confronting him about some inappropriate behavior going on in our home and telling him he needed counseling, he threatened, "If you ever try to leave me, I'll burn the house down." *Does that mean with me and the girls in it?* I wondered. We owned a small plane at the time and a haunting thought kept running through my mind: *Would he crash the plane with all of us on board if he thought I was trying to leave him?* My thoughts weren't all that unrealistic. A couple of years earlier, he killed a dog simply because it wouldn't obey him.

Because I feared the way he might respond if he knew I was unhappy in our marriage, I pretended to be happy. Even though he refused to go to counseling, I committed to staying in the marriage, but not out of love and respect—my commitment was purely fear based.

I started keeping a journal for the first time during that period in my life. That is also when I first began crying out to God. A few years ago I was going to discard the journals, but Joe convinced me to keep them. I'm so glad he did. While Joe and I were writing this book, I decided to reread my journals in an effort to understand where I was spiritually and mentally during that time. It was amazing to look back and see how I was able to excuse the abuse my daughters and I experienced because I was afraid. One entry in my journal reads:

> October 4, 1980: We got into a huge fight today, one of the biggest yet, and he slapped me really hard. He's only done that two times before. Later we talked about it, and he said I pushed him into doing it. I don't know how I feel about that, except that each time we have a really bad fight it gets harder to get over it. He doesn't like to talk about problems, so I feel a lot of things never really get resolved.

Finally, when it became impossible to ignore or excuse the abuse that was going on in our home, I decided to face the fear head-on. After crying out to God for months and trusting Him to get us out of there safely, I gave my husband an ultimatum and honestly didn't care if he burnt the house down or not: "It's counseling or divorce," I said one day after I put my escape plan in place. I had finally decided to inform several close friends in Anchorage and a few people in our little town that I would be confronting my husband about the abuse. He chose divorce. My daughters and I left for California a month later without incident. Because we never had any children of our own, there was no reason to ever have contact with him again.

One thing I've learned through my own experiences and from other women I've spoken with is that abuse and control often feel like protection. As a result, any woman—even ones with strong personalities—can fall victim.

Back in 1980 there was very little help available for victims of abuse. Thankfully times have changed. Now there are agencies— including faith-based organizations—in almost every community that offer support and protection for people in abusive marriages. While some men report being abused by their wives, most domestic violence occurs against women and children. According to a recent fact sheet that collected information from several national organizations, approximately one million women require medical attention each year for injuries inflicted by abusive spouses, and at least half of all abusive husbands also batter their children.[7]

Just because you aren't being physically punched, slapped, or kicked doesn't mean you aren't in an abusive marriage. Here are some questions to ask yourself which will help you determine whether or not you are in an abusive relationship:

- Does my spouse ever try to physically stop me from leaving the room?
- Does my spouse ever push me, grab me or my clothing, or hold me against my will?
- Does my spouse ever tell me to kill myself?
- Does my spouse ever threaten to hurt me for any reason?
- Does my spouse ever point a weapon of any kind toward me, our children, or him or herself?
- Does my spouse ever use language that suggests he or she will "solve" our marriage problems forever through death?
- Am I afraid of my spouse?

These questions are not gender exclusive. If you answered yes to any of them, your marriage is fear based and you are in danger of being a victim of domestic violence. Put a plan together now to get the help you need. If you don't have Internet access, most communities list resources for victims of abuse in the "Community Services" section of their local telephone directories.

If you think your spouse would answer yes to any of the questions because of your behavior, it is never too late to get the help you need to bring the fear level down in your home and save your marriage. But first you must be willing to bring your fear to the light and face it head-on. Confess it to God and be willing to take responsibility to change your ways through counseling and godly accountability. Be willing to physically separate from your spouse and children if you cannot willingly stop the aggressive behavior while getting professional help. As long as your situation remains in the dark, it will be impossible to get the help you, your spouse, and your children need.

What to Do if You Are Being Abused

Tell someone you can trust. If that person doesn't believe you or if you are advised to stay in the abusive situation, then find another person to confide in.

Contact an agency (Christian, if possible) that deals with domestic violence. The agency will help you put a plan together that will get you and your children out of the abusive environment. By getting others involved, you will be able to get help for your spouse as well.

Contact authorities and file a report if your spouse physically touches you or your children or threatens to harm anyone. If your spouse is arrested and has to spend time behind bars, at least counseling will be mandatory.

If your children are being sexually abused in any way, you have a responsibility to tell authorities and seek protection immediately. If you don't, you are breaking the law and you may lose your children once the truth is revealed.

Most important, pray for your spouse and ask others to be praying for your marriage. Then trust God with the outcome of your situation. One thing is certain: If you try to keep the peace when there is domestic violence going on in your home, things will never change. Without help from others, you will eventually fall to pieces, and your spouse and children will fall with you.

Scripture tells us, "Do not be afraid of those who kill the body but cannot kill the soul. Rather, be afraid of the One who can destroy both soul and body in hell. Are not two sparrows sold for a penny? Yet not one of them will fall to the ground apart from the will of your Father. And even the very hairs of your head are all numbered. So don't be afraid; you are worth more than many sparrows" (Matthew 10:28-31).

⤙❧⤛

We have given you several tools in this chapter to help you face the challenges of a fear-based marriage. Some of you will begin putting a plan together now, and you will see the light at the end of the tunnel. But others will read our words and think: *This is easy for them to say; they don't have the spouse I do* or *I've tried to set boundaries in my marriage. It's hopeless* or *I know my marriage is unhealthy, but I'm not willing to put my family through anything that might cause even more pain—like separation.*

If you are thinking similar thoughts or you are unwilling to take the risk to say no to things in your marriage that are immoral, illegal, dangerous, or unhealthy, then you fear your spouse more than God. We once heard a Christian speaker say, "Do it afraid." We are saying the same to you today: Do what you need to do—even if you are afraid. Say what you need to say—even if you are afraid. Have faith in God to give you wisdom as you face the fear in your marriage head-on. This will take self-discipline with a spirit-controlled heart. In the next chapter we will help you to develop these attributes.

GROUP OR SUPPORT-PARTNER DISCUSSION QUESTIONS

1. *Discuss all the reasons that fear is destructive in marriage.*
2. *Discuss the concept of setting healthy boundaries.*
3. *Why are a "soft heart" and gentle spirit important when setting boundaries with your spouse?*
4. *If someone has trouble saying no or hearing no, why would that be a problem in important relationships like marriage?*
5. *Look up and discuss Proverbs 19:18-20.*
6. *What are two or more things you are grateful for?*
7. *Is there anything in your life that requires intercessory prayer (others praying on your behalf)? Share at least one prayer request for yourself and your spouse.*

9

Make Changes— Even with an Unwilling Spouse

If you have faith as small as a mustard seed, you can say to this mountain, Move from here to there, and it will move. Nothing will be impossible for you.

—MATTHEW 17:20

*I*t's true that you can't stop your spouse from filing for a divorce if he or she is determined to end the marriage. But it's a misconception to think that things are hopeless because your spouse isn't willing to work on the marriage as hard as you are—or not at all. We have known countless couples over the years that were just like we were when our marriage was in crisis: They were on and off again, and never on the same page at the same time. Many of them reconciled. Dale and Lori are an example of the power one spouse can have in a crisis marriage.

By the time Dale realized his marriage was in crisis, his wife already had one foot out the door. She wanted her freedom and was unwilling to work on saving their marriage. Dale recalls that time as one of the most significant turning points in his life: "My family, friends, and even some pastors told me there wasn't much hope of saving our marriage if Lori was unwilling to do her part. But I read a small book titled *Saving Your Marriage Alone* by Ed Wheat,[1] and was encouraged to stay committed to the marriage even if Lori wanted to leave. It wasn't as if I'd been a perfect husband up to that point, so I decided to do everything I could to learn how to become a godly husband in the midst of our marriage crisis."

Looking back, Lori admits that she had fallen out of love with Dale and no longer wanted to stay in the marriage. "It would have been so much easier to start over with someone else. I wanted Dale to stop making attempts to save our marriage. I tried to walk out several times, but couldn't bring myself to do it. The reason I couldn't leave was because Dale was growing so close to God and making such positive changes in his life that it made it much harder to walk out on him. I had been raised in religion, but had never known the love of Christ the way Dale was showing it to me. Even though he didn't condone my behavior and had biblical grounds to divorce me at one point, he wasn't judgmental or critical. He just continued to love me, speak the truth, and work on his own relationship with God. Finally, I caved in. How could I walk away from someone who demonstrated that kind of love? Little by little, our relationship was healed and our marriage was saved because my husband chose to work on his own issues and relationship with Christ while waiting for me to repent."

Dale says that his marriage crisis actually drew him closer to God. "I learned to trust Him in a whole new way. Up until our marriage was in crisis, God was 'out there' somewhere, but as I learned to trust Him and lean on His understanding rather than my own, He was right there beside me. I had never known God in that way. With each step of faith, He prepared me for the next. God became real to me, and my love for Lori grew, in spite of her desire to end our marriage."

Today Dale and Lori lead a reconciliation ministry in their church in Modesto, California. The suffering they endured in their own marriage has equipped them to walk alongside those who are in a crisis marriage with an unwilling spouse. They help these abandoned spouses focus on making personal changes, rather than trying to change their mates.

Lori is grateful that their marriage was healed and that God is using them to help others. "We have seen couples reconcile as a result of only one spouse's commitment to God and to their spouse. It's so exciting to watch someone go from hopeless to hopeful. Even in cases where a spouse never repents, we have watched God bless the one who turns to Him in the process."

GOD USES SUFFERING TO PRODUCE HOPE

Contrary to what most people think, it's not a repentant spouse that produces hope in a crisis marriage; it's the suffering that comes from trying to save your marriage alone or waiting for your spouse to repent that allows God to interject hope into your heart. Paul's words are confirmation that God uses suffering as a means to give us hope: "And we rejoice in the hope of the glory of God. Not only so, but we also rejoice in our sufferings, because we know that suffering produces perseverance; perseverance, character; and character, hope. And hope does not disappoint us, because God has poured out his love into our hearts by the Holy Spirit, whom he has given us" (Romans 5:2-5).

The kind of hope Paul was referring to in that passage is the supernatural hope that comes as a result of suffering in a right way—like staying in a marriage that is difficult. Tamara is an example of someone who has developed that kind of hope despite her circumstances.

Stephen wasn't a Christian when Tamara married him more than 14 years ago. She admits now that she was in rebellion against the Lord when she married her drinking buddy. A few months later Tamara became pregnant and, as a result, decided to stop drinking and rededicate her life to Christ. However, her decision was not embraced by Stephen because of the polarization it caused in their opposing lifestyles. As time went on, even though they had two more children, their relationship grew more strained and their marriage was in crisis. At one point, Tamara even suspected that Stephen might be committing adultery and using drugs, although he denied it.

"I asked Stephen to go to counseling with me, but he refused because he doesn't like to talk about problems. This may sound sort of odd, but he aggressively demands peace in our home. He was raised without a dad and his mother never showed him much love. He wants our home to be peaceful and happy all the time, so whenever a topic comes up that might cause a quarrel, he demands that we drop it. That has been so frustrating. One time I decided to go to counseling without him, but the counselor wasn't a Christian and he told me that if Stephen wasn't willing to get counseling and work on his issues, I might as well get a divorce. I'll admit that my original motive for going to the counselor was to have him tell me that our problems were all Stephen's fault. But when he did, I didn't feel released from the marriage by God. Even though my husband has refused to work on our problems, he has always said he loves me, and has been committed to staying in the marriage. I knew God was telling me to stay, but I felt trapped.

"Then one Sunday my pastor asked the congregation a question that changed my life: 'How many of you would be willing to make a commitment to follow the Lord with all your heart, soul, and mind?' I was among those who stood up in response to his question. When I made that commitment, I meant it deep in my heart. As a result, I decided to stop searching for a way out of my marriage. I thought, *How can I love God with all my heart, soul, and mind, and then divorce my husband when he is willing to stay in the marriage no matter what?* Later that week I was really hurting emotionally and I buried my head in a pillow and cried out to God for help. In those moments, it seemed as if I had laid my head on God's lap while He comforted me. A couple of days later while reading the Bible I came across the words, 'well done, good and faithful servant' in Matthew 25:21.

"Those words and the experience of resting in Jesus' lap shifted my thinking from an earthly perspective to an eternal perspective. I knew that it would be foolish to put all my hope in the disposable world we live in. Sure, I might have problems and suffer in a marriage that is difficult. But in terms of eternal life my journey here on earth is short, and more than anything I want to hear the words 'Well done' from the Lord.

"From that point on, I started focusing on what I needed to change through reading books on marriage, taking a marriage reconciliation class, and participating in one-on-one discipleship to become a better wife. I'm not saying that if I knew for sure my husband was unfaithful or he was involved in drugs that I wouldn't make him leave the home. But for some reason, God has never let me know for sure, and I'm not willing to end my marriage on a maybe. I wish God would completely fix my marriage, but I guess right now, God is still fixing me."

~⊙~

Since we have been in ministry, I (Michelle) have spoken with countless women who have been able to change the atmosphere in their homes and marriages just by adopting an eternal perspective the way Tamara has. In many cases, I've even witnessed marriages healed and husbands becoming Christians and godly leaders in their homes. Of course, I have also witnessed women whose husbands not only refused to change, but opted for divorce and moved out. Even so, the women who stayed focused on God and worked on their own problems have had an amazing peace about them in the midst of an unwanted divorce. Denise is an example of a woman who discovered peace amidst a stormy marriage.

Denise was devastated when she discovered her husband was having an affair. Even though Martin was controlling and emotionally immature in the years leading up to his affair, Denise believed that he had a strong commitment to her and their marriage; that is, until she found out about the other woman. "I was so numb after finding out about the affair. I was in a fog for months. The only thing on my mind at first was how I could get Martin to stay in our marriage and not choose to be with the other woman. I'm not a quitter and I had always believed our marriage would get better the longer we were married. But when I realized Martin might leave, it caused me to start praying to God for help.

"I know He heard my prayers because soon after, a neighbor invited me to join a small women's group that began meeting in her home. It turned out that the material she had chosen to use focused on how to be a godly wife and mother, even in the midst of stressful circumstances. I'd never studied the Bible before and when I read Proverbs 14:1, 'The wise woman builds her house, but with her own hands the foolish one tears hers down,' I made a commitment to be wise and keep my family together even though I knew adultery was a biblical reason for divorce. My husband eventually broke off his affair, but he was never really repentant. Even so, I continued to work on being a godly wife and attend the women's group.

"I wish I could say that my husband has come to the Lord as a result of my decision to follow Christ and stay committed to our marriage, but his immature behavior has never changed. Even though the venom he spews during our disagreements hurts deeply, I honestly feel more sadness for him because I know he needs God. Recently Martin told me that he wants a divorce. I suspected this was coming because lately when I've tried to kiss him, his lips are cold and he doesn't respond. But even though our marriage has been in crisis for the past ten years, I wouldn't trade the relationship I have with the Lord as a result. My suffering drew me to God and if my unbelieving husband wants to leave, I won't try to stop him this time. Yes, I'm sad that Martin doesn't want to work hard to have a great marriage, but I'm at peace. Marriage is not for wimps and God taught me how to bloom in a difficult marriage, so I'm sure He can teach me to have joy in what lies ahead."

GOD USES SUFFERING TO PRODUCE CHANGE

I (Joe) talk with guys all the time who say the suffering they experienced in their marriages was the wake-up call that caused them to make changes they should have made years earlier. The Bible is full of examples where God has used pain and suffering to get people to realize their need for Him and make lasting changes in their lives. Here's a story that I heard years ago that's a great parallel to the measures God sometimes uses to get our attention: A stagecoach driver was carrying a young woman and her small daughter over snow-covered terrain. When the driver glanced back to check on his passengers, he noticed that the woman had taken off her winter coat and put it over her daughter to keep her warm. They had both fallen asleep and he knew they would soon freeze to death if he didn't take action. The driver yanked the reigns on the stagecoach and jumped down. Grabbing the child from her mother's arms, he threw the woman into the snow. In horror, the woman watched the stagecoach take off with the driver holding her daughter in his arms. Yelling and screaming as loud as she could, she began running after the stagecoach waving her arms and begging the driver to stop.

A few moments later the driver stopped and waited for her to catch up. She was out of breath and wet with sweat and tears. When he handed the child back to her mother and put his arms around them both, the woman cried, "Why did you do such a cruel and painful thing to me?" He answered, "Because, I knew you were dying. Running away with your daughter was the only thing I could think of that was severe enough for you to wake up and do what was needed to save you both."

God's ways of getting our attention are sometimes a lot like that stagecoach driver. You can probably look back at many situations in your life that seemed painful at the time, but God used these circumstances as His wake-up call to draw you closer to Him. I jokingly remind the guys in my Thursday-night group that marriage is a three-ring ceremony: First comes the engagement ring, then comes the wedding ring, and last comes the "suffer–ring." Even though the guys chuckle when I say it, we all know it's true. Marriage is difficult and God expects husbands and wives to suffer—His way—for each other. When we complain and focus on what's wrong with everyone else, we end up suffering because of our own self-centered thinking. But that kind of suffering isn't God's will: "If you suffer, it should not be as a murderer or thief or any other kind of criminal, or even as a meddler. . . . So then, those who suffer according to God's will should commit themselves to their faithful Creator and continue to do good" (1 Peter 4:15, 19).

Michelle and I can look back now and see what God was doing during our painful marriage crisis. It's an added blessing to know that the suffering we experienced back then wasn't in vain because we can now help others find hope. God promises in His Word that if you suffer because of doing what's right, He restores your painful times: "And the God of all grace, who called you to his eternal glory in Christ, after you have suffered a little while, will himself restore you and make you strong, firm and steadfast" (1 Peter 5:10).

CHANGE REQUIRES SELF-DISCIPLINE

Several months before we reconciled, I (Michelle) heard a Christian counselor on the radio discussing troubled marriages. He said, "I can offer hope and major changes in any marriage if you just give me one willing spouse—the one with the most self-discipline." He also said it was unrealistic to think that both spouses would have the same amount of willingness or self-discipline to make positive changes if they had severe marriage problems or were separated.

Until that moment it had never occurred to me that a husband and wife didn't have to work on their marriage as a couple in order to make major changes in the home. Although I had been learning to trust God and rest in the arms of Jesus, I was still reacting negatively to almost everything Joe said or did. We were in a war of wills in our crisis marriage, and if Joe said something that I thought was unfair, controlling, manipulative, or sarcastic, I'd fire back with words designed to regain a position of strength in our battle. After each argument I would survey my emotional wounds incurred as a result of our bantering and prepare for the next round. My preparation for future fights consisted of focusing on all the ways Joe had been unfair and waiting for him to apologize. *After all,* I would think, *how can we improve our marriage if he isn't willing to be the spiritual leader and change first?* I definitely wasn't practicing self-control or self-discipline, and I continued to believe that as long as Joe wasn't willing to take responsibility for his part of our marriage troubles, things would remain hopeless; that is, until I heard the counselor's advice on the radio program that night. Suddenly, I felt hopeful. I realized that I could actually change the negative things in my life even if Joe was unwilling to do his part.

I'm not saying that I repented of my hard heart toward Joe at that moment—I didn't. In fact, it was several months before my heart softened toward him. What did happen, though, was a paradigm shift in my thinking. My focus shifted from focusing on Joe's faults to changing my own. That was a huge turning point and a necessary ingredient for lasting change that had been lacking throughout my life, even after becoming a Christian.

Of course, knowing it in my head and actually acting on that knowledge were two very different things. I wasn't even sure what I needed to change at first. But as I prayed and asked God to reveal areas that I needed to work on, He was more than happy to reveal them to me. Some areas that required change were: having patience with other people's children, working projects through to completion, taking better care of my body, responding kindly to rude or incompetent store clerks, being courteous to other drivers, and a whole lot more. As I worked on being more self-disciplined and less reactive, I noticed that my heart softened toward others—including Joe.

～◎～

As I said earlier, Michelle was my "little god" when we first married and I liked it when she was focused on me. But as with all false gods, they eventually let you down and leave you hopeless. The "Serenity Prayer," which many people in recovery ministries are familiar with, explains the importance of accepting the things in life that you can't change, changing the things that you can, and having the wisdom to know the difference. Most of the people we talk to who are in a crisis marriage with a spouse who is unwilling to do his or her part feel hopeless because they haven't yet grasped this concept.

Consider this example: Imagine that you are renting a furnished three-bedroom, two-bath home in a fairly nice neighborhood, but there are a lot of things wrong with your home: The faucet leaks; the toilet is always running; the refrigerator keeps food cold only on the top shelf; the yard is a mess; the fence needs new paint; the interior walls are covered with old wallpaper; the carpets and all the flooring are stained; the curtains are old; and the couch is soiled.

But the rent is only $250 a month.

The deal you made with the landlord was that you would rent the home "as is." When you first moved in, you thought you could live with the bleak surroundings, but as the months go by you realize the atmosphere is bringing you down. You are probably thinking, *Well, with such a great deal on the rent, and since the neighborhood is decent, I could just hire the work that needs to be done, or do the work myself to fix the place up!*

But here's the catch: The landlord has told you that he will only fix what is required by law, and that you can't make any changes to the walls, fence, floors, or appliances. Nor can you move any of the soiled furniture out.

Perhaps due to these problems with the rental, you are now thinking, *Well, forget that. I'll just move then.*

Moving would certainly be an option, but to rent a three-bedroom, two-bath home in that same neighborhood would run you about $1,300. And if you did move, you would no longer have extra money to do anything, and you'd probably have to get a second job.

Would you become hopeless? Or would you change the things you could change in order to be content where you were? The apostle Paul said, "I have leaned to be content whatever the circumstances" (Philippians 4:11).

The truth is, if you lived in a house that needed fixing and the landlord refused to do his or her part you could still . . .

- plant lots of shrubs and flowers outdoors to take the focus off the shabby fence;
- buy furniture coverings and decorative items;

- put some great looking wall hangings over the chipped paint;
- pull the curtains aside and insert blinds or shutters to let in the sun;
- place lots of palms and house plants for beauty;
- and put nice area rugs over the carpet and floors.

By doing these things, you would camouflage your drab surroundings and create an atmosphere you could enjoy. Would these changes require an investment? Definitely. Change does require us to give of ourselves, and in this case, fixing up a rental would probably cost you a little money and time, but it would be well worth it. Of course, if the home became a dangerous place to live (ceiling falling, roof leaking, fire hazards, etc.) your landlord would have to willingly fix it, or be forced to by law—or you could move.

Likewise, if your marriage needs fixing and you have an unwilling spouse, you will have to take responsibility to change the things in the marriage that you can, and let go of the rest. Possible changes you can make include:

- attending a same-gender Bible study in order to meet other Christians and grow in your knowledge of the Lord;
- seeking to make same-gender friends that have the same interests in order to enjoy activities when your spouse is not available; (Be careful not to spend too much time away from home, however. Remember that balance is always important.)
- taking a class to learn better communication skills;
- signing up for a class in something you are interested in so you can develop your natural God-given talents;
- exercising and eating right so you can feel better and be attractive for your spouse;
- saying nice things about your spouse and family in order to develop a healthier mental attitude toward others.

While making these types of changes may not necessarily cost you financially, they will require an investment on your part. However, isn't your life worth it? By doing these things, you would be able to grow spiritually, mentally, and physically and learn to enjoy life regardless of your spouse. A spouse who enjoys life is much more attractive than one who is sulking or pathetic because things seem hopeless. Of course, just as in the imagined landlord situation, if your marriage becomes dangerous, your spouse would have to fix that behavior either willingly or by force—or you could move.

SELF-NURTURING CAN PRODUCE JOY AND TAKE PRESSURE OFF OTHERS

Most couples whose marriages are in crisis seem to lose a sense of themselves as individuals. (This was true for Michelle and me.) The stress of marriage troubles and urgent demands of the day often replace the simple enjoyments in life. We refer to this as "self-nurturing." People who are not self-nurtured will tend to be self-centered because they will either have unrealistic expectations of others to meet their needs (self-centered thinking), or they will be running around saying they are too busy to self-nurture because everyone else needs them (which is also a form of self-centered thinking).

If you have never spent regular time alone just enjoying the world God created for you, or if you thought marriage meant that you no longer should or could spend any time by yourself, you have bought into a lie from the Enemy. God expects us to enjoy the life He has given us. Beware of using the excuse that you don't have enough time to take care of yourself because that's another lie. God has given each of us the same amount of time in the day. If you aren't taking responsibility to meet your own needs and keep yourself rested and joyful, you won't be able to meet the needs of others as God intended.

Notice that Paul doesn't tell us *not* to care for ourselves when he instructs Christians to look out for each other: "Each of you should look not only to your own interests, but also to the interests of others. Your attitude should be the same as that of Christ Jesus" (Philippians 2:4-5).

Self-Nurturing Is Not Self-Centered

Throughout the New Testament, we see Jesus caring for Himself many times, even before giving to others. He spent hours praying alone, He left multitudes to go to another region, and He ate and rested often during His three-year ministry on earth. Through His individual time alone with God and the care He took for His body (the Temple), He was able to more effectively meet the needs of others.

I (Michelle) took a class at our community college in 1988 while Joe and I were separated. One of my first assignments was to make a list of activities I could do alone that were not illegal or expensive. I added "not immoral" to the criteria as well. The list became one of my self-discipline exercises during our separation, and after we reconciled Joe and I named it the "Self-Nurture List." Now we each have our own list and still implement weekly activities in order to stay self-nurtured. We also use these lists as a tool to help people who are in crisis marriages. It's surprising how many times individuals have told us that self-nurturing changed their attitudes and brought joy and contentment back into their lives. Some have even credited the implementation of self-nurturing activities as a turning point in their crisis marriages.

Make a Self-Nurture List

Make a list of 10-20 activities that you enjoy doing *alone* that are not immoral, illegal, or expensive. Then, beginning today, implement at least one activity into your life each day. The whole idea of engaging in these activities alone is that they provide an opportunity to completely relax without trying to accommodate anyone else's needs. Once you regularly practice self-nurturing, and if your spouse agrees, join your lists and do some of the activities together. For instance, Joe and I both have yard sales and riding bikes on our lists and we enjoy doing those things together. Some examples are:

1. Reading
2. Walking
3. Biking
4. Fishing
5. Going to movies
6. Playing or watching a sport that is not expensive
7. Window shopping
8. Yard sales
9. Listening to or playing music
10. Going for a latte or ice cream
11. _____
12. _____
13. _____
14. _____
15. _____
16. _____
17. _____
18. _____
19. _____
20. _____

Here are other steps that you can take without your spouse's participation:

1. Admit that your marriage needs help. Many people who are in troubled marriages are in denial or afraid to admit their marriages need help—even to their spouses. Recently I (Michelle) facilitated a group in our community for women who wanted to strengthen their marriage. Each woman introduced herself, and many shared they had great marriages and were just there to make them even better. Only a handful admitted that they were there because of troubled marriages. As the weeks went on, however, and trust built among the women, it turned out that more than half were silently suffering in a crisis marriage but didn't want to tell anyone. That wasn't as surprising as the fact that in some of the cases, their spouses didn't even know.

Are you and your spouse on the same page when it comes to the health of your marriage? Maybe you think your spouse is refusing to make changes, but in reality, he or she doesn't even think your marriage is in crisis. We have heard many people say that even though their spouses ranted and raved or threatened to leave in the midst of an argument, they had not labeled their marriages as "crisis marriages." Sadly, because many people are raised in homes where unhealthy marriages are modeled—or with no model at all—they think daily arguing and lack of intimacy are acceptable and even normal. Following are some descriptions of marriages in different stages. Without input from your spouse, use a separate sheet of paper and list the numbers of the statements that best describe your marriage:

1. Arguments happen, but I love my spouse. I do not feel hopeless and I am committed to our marriage.

2. Quarrels are left unresolved and I am frustrated by our inability to discuss important issues.

3. There is a lack of sexual intimacy in our marriage.

4. I secretly entertain thoughts of separation or divorce and imagine what life would be like if I were married to someone else or not married at all.

5. In the midst of arguments, one or both of us voice threats of separation or divorce.

6. I feel hopeless and worn out from trying to keep our marriage together and my spouse isn't trying to help.

7. There is abusive behavior going on in our home.

8. Things look pretty hopeless because we are separated and divorce is a strong possibility (or is pending).

After you have made your list, prayerfully ask your spouse to do the same. If you both listed only the first statement, you can assume your marriage is not in crisis, but don't get so comfortable that you neglect to continue doing your part to keep it healthy.

All the other statements are ones we regularly hear when couples are in crisis or have separated. If either of you listed any of the other numbers, your marriage needs help.

If your spouse gets angry (remember to use the tools in previous chapters when discussing 'hot topics' and boundaries) and refuses to complete this exercise, just let it go and accept that your marriage is in crisis with an unwilling spouse.

2. Let go of victim thinking. We will all suffer in this world. In John 16:33 Jesus said that we would have trouble. How one person is able to get through trials and use the trouble to help others while another falls into hopelessness depends on how each person processes his or her pain. One way the Enemy spreads hopelessness is by tempting people to entertain thoughts designed to make them feel like victims. That's what happened to Rose.

"When my husband moved out almost four years ago, it was a real shock. We had been in counseling because of some problems I was struggling with as a result of childhood abuse. Scott was so committed to standing beside me while we worked on the problems together that I honestly believed he would never leave. We attended church together and he even served in a leadership role. When he left, he did so in a way that turned my world upside down. He had planned to leave for weeks and secretly pulled money out of our bank accounts. I had no idea of Scott's plans. The pain of him leaving, and the way in which he did it, created a perfect foothold for the Enemy.

All I could think of was that I had become a victim all over again of someone I loved and trusted. Looking back, I can see how I had actually become of victim of my own negative thinking.

"Finally, when the suffering became so great that I didn't think I could bear it any longer, God revealed the truth to me through a speaker who came to our church. The visiting pastor spoke about 'victim thinking,' and through his message I realized that my thoughts were not focused on God—instead they were focused on what others had done to me. While I couldn't change the childhood abuse or what my husband had done, the message and scriptures the pastor shared that weekend helped me understand that I had given in to Satan's ploy to take away my joy as God's child. That weekend, using what I learned from the pastor, I started making changes. I decided to think about things that were true, noble, right, pure, lovely and admirable, based on Philippians 4:8. It wasn't easy at first, but as time went on, thinking positive thoughts based on God and His Word replaced my habits of negative thinking. Even my friends and family noticed a difference in my countenance. I'm still heartbroken about my marriage situation, but that doesn't mean I can't have the joy of the Lord while I wait for what God has in store next, and use my past to help others!"

3. Become proactive. The following exercises are designed to practice proactive behavior. Because you can decide to have patience beforehand, rather than allowing these stressful situations to happen unexpectedly, these are a great way to learn patience and practice self-control:

- Every so often, go to a store or restaurant that normally has rude or incompetent help. Decide beforehand that you will remain calm, courteous, and godly in your interactions. If possible, address the person helping you by name and try to give a genuine compliment when leaving.

- Look for at least one opportunity every week to get in the longest line at the grocery store, bank, or traffic. Instead of complaining and grumbling, decide to pray silently for the people you see while you wait. (You may never know the pain and suffering that the person you are praying for is going through.)

- Call or visit a relative or family friend with whom it is difficult to spend time; perhaps someone with a pessimistic attitude about life or someone who wants to do all the talking. Spend time listening and being genuinely interested in what they have to say (it's easier than you think when you are being Spirit-led). When you hang up or leave, practice self-control by not complaining about the visit with others.

- You may laugh at this, but it really is something we have used to practice self-control and patience: If your family watches television, take turns weekly letting others in your home have complete charge of the remote control. Sit quietly while he or she surfs the channels and decide beforehand that when you hear half sentences and miss the end of a movie, you won't complain.

- Volunteer to serve in an area in your church or community in which you normally don't serve, such as providing food to the homeless, greeting at church, teaching a class, visiting nursing homes or those in the hospital, sending cards to those suffering, etc.

- Decide not to honk your car horn unless it is to avoid an accident—which of course is its purpose. This is more difficult than you think and is a great way to practice self- and spirit-control. Praying for other drivers who make mistakes is better than honking and shaking your fists—especially if you have one of those Christian symbols or the name of your church on your car.

4. Obey God. Obedience to God is a weapon that Satan hates because it builds our Christian character and ability to witness to others. Lisa is an example of someone who has been able to maintain her sweet spirit and witness to others even though her marriage has been in a crisis for years. "Once it became clear that I was the only one willing to work on our marriage, I had a choice to think negative thoughts and have a hard heart or think about the Lord and pray for God's grace and a soft heart. I call it my 'self-talk.' I'm sad that my husband doesn't choose to work on our marriage, but I'm not bitter. I've simply discovered that when I do what's right, and think good thoughts to avoid harboring bitterness, I'm a better person for it—and so is my husband."

∽᙭∾

If you feel that your marriage is one-sided and you are the only one working to save it, we want to encourage you to hang in there and continue persevering. Make your self-nurture list and do everything you can to become a better person in the midst of your crisis. Regardless of what your spouse chooses to do, you will still have to stand alone before God one day and account for the ways you used the gift of life that He gave you. Keep the eternal perspective and grow in your walk with Him.

GROUP OR SUPPORT-PARTNER DISCUSSION QUESTIONS

1. Discuss how God has used a past circumstance or a current one to produce hope in your life.

2. Why is self-discipline important in marriage?

3. *Discuss your self-nurture list.*
4. *What are some things that individuals can do to make their marriages better when they have an unwilling spouse?*
5. *Look up and discuss 2 Peter 1:4-7.*
6. *Share anything you are thankful for in your life.*
7. *Share a prayer request.*

10

Listen to the Right Counsel

Therefore I urge you, brethren, by the mercies of God, to
present your bodies a living and holy sacrifice, acceptable
to God, which is your spiritual service of worship.

—ROMANS 12:1 NASB

When Joe and I were separated the second time, before we
renewed our vows, I had become friends with a woman
at church who seemed to know a lot about the Bible. One day a conversation came up about divorce and remarriage. She told me that
God recognized only first marriages and that I should reconcile with
my first husband.

"Do you mean I should divorce Joe?" I asked her.

"Yes, because you should have never married him to begin with,"
she answered.

I had just started attending church and since she had been a believer
for so long, I accepted what she said. However, a couple of days later,
while discussing her advice with a pastor, he explained that God wanted
me to remain in the marriage I was in now (see 1 Corinthians 7:20 and
surrounding verses). The pastor also warned me about the dangers of
getting counsel from only one source, even if the person is a Christian.

It's true that God looks favorably on having His children rely on more than one counselor: "Where there is no guidance the people fall, But in abundance of counselors there is victory" (Proverbs 11:14 NASB). But God also desires balance (see Proverbs 11:1), and having too many counselors can be just as damaging. That's what happened in Sam's case.

Sam worked in a Christian organization and was very involved in his church. He was also an outgoing guy with a lot of friends. When his wife started having an affair and demanded he move out so she could move the other man in, all his friends rallied around him with godly counsel and support. The problem was, they were all giving him different advice. Sam was frustrated and confused by the time he called our ministry. "Some tell me to love my wife unconditionally and to remain in the home; others say to set boundaries and make *her* leave. One man told me that under no circumstance should I take the kids from her if we separate, and yet others say not to subject the kids to her adulterous lifestyle and that I should fight for full custody!"

Sam had too many counselors and had become bogged down with too much advice. I (Joe) suggested he narrow his advice circle to no more than five people and I helped him put together a support system that was manageable. Sam's wife did move out and left their two children in his care. Although he has been through a painful time, Sam credits his small support system for his ability to remain steadfast and calm during his crisis. He also believes that if he had kept listening to the masses, he would have given up in despair. "I was confused because everyone's advice sounded good and most of it sounded godly, but there was no way I could have applied all of it, even if I'd wanted to."

ᦂ

Throughout the years we have watched people on both ends of the spectrum—those refusing to ask for advice and those running to and fro asking advice from anyone who would listen. We were guilty of doing this as well. It's important to have balance when seeking advice in order to make wise decisions for yourself and your marriage, especially if you are working on your relationship without your spouse.

If you've ever had a serious illness, or even just a common cold, you've probably noticed that the well-meaning "advice givers" come out of the woodwork. Since most of the remedies contradict each other, applying all of them at once would probably kill you. The wise thing to do is to create an advice circle consisting of a few health-care professionals and those who have experienced your same ailment, and then apply what would work best concerning your particular illness and situation.

Likewise, when your marriage is "sick," if you try to apply every bit of counsel—even godly advice—you will probably kill the marriage. The misconception that couples or individuals in crisis should listen to and apply every bit of godly counsel they receive is a recipe for confusion, not reconciliation. Instead, create an advice circle as you would when treating an illness. Using the principles of God, gather a few mature people and an expert or two, add those who have experienced your same situation, and then apply the advice that works best for your marriage.

We have given you several tools throughout the book that will help you reconcile your marriage and remain hopeful, regardless of what your spouse does. But just like avoiding certain medicines or activities if you are ill, sometimes what you *don't* do during your crisis is just as important as what you do. Here are some tips to help you get the most from your advice circle as well as avoid making some of the same mistakes we and others have made.

1. Avoid sharing anything that dishonors your spouse. Certainly in professional settings, such as one-on-one counseling with a pastor or therapist, you will need to be totally honest about your marriage and the problems between you and your spouse. In fact, not doing so may hinder you from getting proper advice. But in all other settings, speaking negatively or sharing personal things about your spouse can harm your chances of reconciling. We frequently receive calls from people who are deeply hurt by their spouses' betrayal of confidence. You should not share personal information with anyone else unless you have your spouse's permission to do so *first*. Here are several areas to be especially cautious about when sharing:

- Sexual problems
- Private struggles that your spouse has told you in confidence, or that only the two of you know about (except for abuse or other illegal activities, of course)
- Childhood trauma or abuse that your spouse has not shared publicly
- Past sins that your spouse has confessed and repented of
- Your spouse's fears and vulnerable areas such as: fear of rejection, fear of failure, secret thoughts, etc.
- Anything your spouse has shared in detail during a counseling session
- Negative comments about someone else—especially another family member—that your spouse may have told you in private

There is nothing more hurtful to your spouse than to have him or her discover that you have revealed something that was considered safe and confidential between the two of you. We have even talked with people whose spouses made up lies in an effort to destroy their reputation in the church or community. Regardless of gender or temperament, anyone who has ever been betrayed by the person with whom he or she was once "supernaturally one" will tell you that those wounds ran deep and took a long time to heal.

If you have been guilty of sharing things about your spouse which should have been kept confidential, confess those things to the Lord and ask Him to give you the self-control to change in this area and not to fall prey to this temptation again. "He who conceals a transgression seeks love, But he who repeats a matter separates intimate friends" (Proverbs 17:9 NASB).

2. *Avoid forcing your family and friends to take sides.* This was an area in which I (Michelle) made a huge mistake. Each time Joe and I separated, I was certain our marriage would end in divorce. After all, it wasn't as if I had never gone through a divorce and couldn't recognize a hopeless situation when I saw one. As I had done in the past, getting support from family and friends was important, and convincing them to take my side helped justify why reconciliation was impossible. Only by God's grace did I keep my complaints about Joe to things that were based on our inability to communicate and our incessant arguing, rather than trying to think up ways to destroy his reputation or malign his character. Nevertheless, I did complain about how unhappy Joe made me in an effort to convince others that divorce was our only option. Consequently, when we reconciled the last time, my family and even some friends were skeptical and had a negative view of Joe that was hard for them to overcome. It took some family members several years to trust that reconciling with Joe was a wise decision.

We have known many couples who reconciled only to have to overcome the same problem again. Some created unhealthy advice circles designed to reject their spouses rather than reconcile. Others even quoted professionals and leading marriage experts in order to convince family and friends (and those trying to help—like us) that their marriage problems were not their fault. Through the years, we've heard comments like: "Even my Christian counselor thinks our situation is hopeless and that my spouse will never be able to connect emotionally" or "The group facilitator at our church agrees that these kinds of addictions never go away and my spouse will always go back to his addiction" or "My Christian friend says that my spouse fits the profile of an abuser and will never change or be safe to reconcile with."

More than once we have heard repentant spouses who wanted to reconcile admit they had exaggerated details in their crisis marriages in order to build emotional support and allegiance. Sadly, many of these admissions came too late and their marriages ended in divorce.

Think about the ways you have been talking about your spouse lately. Are you sharing your marriage problems and/or stretching the truth about your spouse in an effort to get your family and friends to side with you?

⚬⚬⚬

I (Joe) often put a large plastic baby-bottle piggy bank in the center of the table in my Thursday-night men's group. Every time someone complains about his wife, I make him put a quarter in the "cry-baby" bottle. It allows for humor, and still holds all of them (including myself) accountable. Maybe you will need to come up with something like the "cry-baby" bottle to help break your habit of speaking negatively about your spouse. Ask your support partner to help hold you accountable as well.

Most of us have problems saying positive things about people who have hurt us, but God calls us to speak well of each other. He warns us about causing division—especially against our spouses (see Ephesians 5:19-25). As we have stated throughout this book, do your best to pray for your spouse and to show respect, regardless of what he or she is doing. Chances are you will reconcile, and when you do, you will not have the difficult task of trying to change everyone's negative views about your spouse because of what you have said.

3. *Avoid forming an advice circle that feeds your roller-coaster emotions.* If your spouse has just dropped a bombshell of some kind

and/or wants out of the marriage, your emotions will probably be all over the place, changing daily, if not hourly. One moment you may sob, "I can't live without my spouse!" You may want to cling, begging him or her not to leave. The next moment, you may want your spouse out of your life for good. Through gritted teeth and newfound confidence you mumble, "Who needs him [or her] anyway!"

But emotions in the beginning of a marriage crisis cannot be trusted. You should never make lasting decisions in that state of mind. That's why it is important to get advice from people who won't feed your roller-coaster emotions and are grounded in the Word of God.

In his book *Hope for the Separated*, Gary Chapman writes: "During separation, individuals are emotionally pulled in two directions. . . . A person may sincerely think one thing today and something else tomorrow. He is not intending to lie. He is simply reporting his feelings at the moment. It is to be hoped that he or she will learn not to make decisions based upon feelings but upon what is right."[1]

Your advice circle needs to be one that can help bring balance to your life when you swing from one emotion to another. For instance, if you are feeling hopeless and wonder how you can go on without your spouse, your advice circle can help point you in the direction of self-nurture activities or help you stay connected with others. Engaging in activities that nurture you sends the message to your spouse that you are not so dependent on whether or not he or she returns home.

On the other hand, if you are happy to be rid of your spouse and are feeling a sense of freedom, your advice circle can help you stay focused on God and the things you need to work on in order to save the marriage. Keeping focused on God sends a message to your spouse that you are open to reconciliation and are not counting the days until you can replace him or her with someone new.

4. Avoid "diagnosing" your spouse. There seems to be a newly discovered diagnosis or disorder around every corner these days. We don't mean to make light of those who suffer from a legitimate disorder, mental illness, or chronic condition and have had to seek treatment to deal with their problem effectively. Sometimes immature behavior can also look like a disorder. For instance, a spouse who is happy one moment but throws a tantrum the next might look like a manic-depressive person. But in reality, that person may just have a problem with immature, self-centered behavior. As we mentioned earlier, some behavior is learned and can be unlearned in a matter of weeks once the desire to change takes over. But those decisions are usually a result of maturity and/or spiritual growth.

Sometimes personality quirks that can be improved with a few helpful behavior tips can seem like disorders. We know several men and women who have "diagnosed" their spouses and demanded they take medication based on a television show, a newly published book out on the market, the latest fad, or advice from friends. The sad thing is that even some professional counselors are quick to diagnose and medicate rather than provide people with the tools they need in order to change and set healthy boundaries.

One couple we know made an appointment with a Christian counselor to get advice on how to handle their teenage son's disrespect. The husband wasn't too keen on attending counseling and felt their son was just going through normal teenage self-centeredness. He thought some old-fashion discipline could take care of the problem. But since the daily news was full of teens who had harmed and even killed classmates and he wanted to quiet his wife's fears, the husband agreed to go to counseling. The first week the couple went to the counselor without their son. The next two weeks they brought their son with them, even though all he did during each session was sulk and refuse to talk. The fourth week, the husband told his wife if she wanted to continue taking their son it was fine with him, but he just didn't see how forcing their son to sit through the appointments was doing any good. The wife decided to go to the next appointment alone.

When she showed up at the counselor's office without her husband and son, the counselor suggested that perhaps the husband might be suffering from a social disorder, causing him to be unable to connect deeply with others, including their son, and that was the reason the teen was behaving rudely. When the wife asked the counselor's advice as to what could be done about her husband's "disorder," the counselor suggested medication. The wife left the office that day a little confused. She wondered if the counselor was right and she had just been blind to her husband's "disorder" all those years. She decided to monitor her husband's behavior for a few weeks before telling him what the counselor said.

For the next couple of weeks, whenever her husband was tired, moody, or overworked, behavior previously considered normal was now viewed as symptomatic of some "hidden disorder" that had gone unnoticed all those years. He had obviously passed this disorder down to their son, she thought. A couple of weeks later, our friend finally told her husband what the counselor had said. After the initial "you've-got-to-be-kidding" conversation, they both saw the humor in what had happened. This incident occurred several years ago. Their son grew out of his rude behavior soon after they set healthy boundaries in their home. As for her husband's "social disorder," the couple jokingly admits that it still pops up now and then when the husband is tired or has had a stressful day at work.

If you suspect that your spouse (or child) really does suffer from a social or mental disorder, spend time in prayer and get more than one diagnosis if possible. And don't forget to implement healthy boundaries along with behavior modification techniques as part of the treatment.

5. Avoid comparing your marriage with the marriages of others. We all covet to some extent. Our culture is subtly and carefully crafted toward keeping people dissatisfied in order to keep the economy going. Our house isn't big enough, our car isn't good enough, and our things aren't new enough. Even in desiring a good marriage, we can fall into the trap of coveting what someone else has. We can look at another couple and want their marriage (or one of them!) just as easily as wanting their possessions.

Several years ago, soon after we reconciled and started serving in ministry together, Joe and I conducted a class at our church using one of the videotaped series from leading Christian marriage expert Gary Smalley. Sometime that year, about the sixth time that we had used the series, I realized I was feeling resentment toward Joe. *After all,* I thought, *Joe has watched these videos at least a half dozen times and he still isn't saying and doing the things Gary does for his wife!* Over the weeks, I listened carefully to all the things that Gary Smalley said to do in order to have a great marriage, all the while secretly stewing because Joe wasn't doing everything exactly as Gary said he should. Little by little, I started noticing more and more things in our marriage that I was dissatisfied with and imagined what it would be like to have a "perfect Smalley marriage."

My discontentment soon began to show. I interjected little negative comments and instead of reaching for Joe's hand while the videos were showing, I sat with my arms folded, glaring at him out of the corner of my eye. Every week I waited for Joe to ask me to rate our marriage. (According to Smalley, the husband should ask the wife to rate the marriage since she tends to be more honest than he does about the health of the marriage.) A rating of "10" indicates a perfect marriage. The first time we watched the videos, I was prepared to rate our marriage a "9" when Joe asked, but by the sixth viewing it had dropped down to "0" in my book.

Not only was I wanting Joe to ask me to rate our marriage, I was also waiting for him to ask me what was wrong. "A man should be sensitive to his wife and ask her how he can make their marriage a '10,'" Gary said. I decided that if I had to tell Joe I was upset, it simply didn't count . . . he had to recognize it all by himself and ask me how I was feeling!

One day, in his frustration with my behavior, Joe asked if I had a problem with him. "Yes, as a matter of fact, I do," I said, relieved that he had finally noticed and asked. Joe had the most amazed expression on his face as I unleashed weeks of frustration over the fact that he hadn't done everything suggested on the videos and that he wasn't more like Gary Smalley.

When I was through, Joe looked me square in the eyes and quipped, "Michelle, if I were more like Gary Smalley, I'd be so popular that I'd be traveling all over the countryside doing seminars and I'd never be home with you!"

His words brought me back to reality. In all my imagining, I hadn't really thought about the fact that no marriage is perfect and the idea of wanting our marriage to look exactly like someone else's wasn't even realistic or pleasing to God.

✧

A few years after that incident, Michelle and I conducted a workshop at a marriage conference. Gary Smalley and his two sons were also giving a workshop at the same conference. When their workshop was over, I walked up to Gary and with a smile on my face said, "I have a bone to pick with you," and then told him the story. We all had a good laugh. He and his sons assured Michelle and me that there was no such thing as a "perfect Smalley marriage."

6. *Avoid "cookie cutter" solutions.* A Christian speaker once said, "If

five women who were married to alcoholic husbands all came to me for counsel, I would tell each one to go spend a few days in prayer, read God's Word, and wait to get some sort of direction from Him. Then I would give them counsel. I guarantee you that all five of those women would come back to me with different answers as to how they should proceed with their alcoholic husband."

The point the speaker was making, and we have discovered this as well, is that there is no easy "cookie cutter" solution for marriages in crisis. There are so many factors to consider that it would be impossible for a counselor or advice circle to give couples or individuals a one-stop recipe for reconciliation. We tell pastors and leaders that the best thing they can do to bring down the divorce rate in their churches is to have a "first-response team" in place with different methods to respond immediately to couples in crisis, and provide them with what they need based on each persons or couple's individual situation. People who expect one book, one seminar, one counselor, or one method to be a cure-all for a crisis marriage set themselves up for disappointment—which is what the Enemy wants.

One time I (Michelle) read a book that was "guaranteed" to keep any marriage affair-proof. The book was written by a woman who claimed to have a great marriage and wanted to share all the ways she kept their romance alive. There were definitely good tips in that book, some that I still use today. However, there's one tip that I'll never use with Joe again.

The author suggested "kidnapping" your husband at lunch (with his boss's permission, of course). Then, after telling your husband that he isn't going back to work, you blindfold him, put him in the backseat of your car, and drive him to your favorite out-of-town getaway. That might work for some men or women, but Joe hated it. Not only did he not like being told that he couldn't go back to work—knowing he would have double the work waiting the next day—but anyone who knows me also knows I get lost a lot and Joe doesn't like being a passenger when I'm driving. Why I thought he would like being blindfolded in the backseat of our car while I attempted to get us somewhere in another town escapes me. We had driven only 20 minutes before Joe ripped off the blindfold and ruined the "romantic" adventure. Then, because I made reservations at a hotel, we got into an argument about how much this "surprise" was going to cost. When it was all said and done, I realized that not all romantic tips work with every person.

❧

I (Joe) have retold that attempted adventure story several times. It's a perfect example of how we expect what someone else has done to work for us. We laugh about our "romantic" adventure now, but Michelle's right. . . . I hated it. I like to be spontaneous, as I've said before, but that whole idea bordered on crazy, as far as I was concerned.

❧

One way to avoid "cookie cutter" dates or formulas in your marriage is to find out what your spouse likes and dislikes. Michelle and I created this tool to use when we want to surprise each other and also enjoy the experience ourselves. We have found that even when couples are separated, this exercise can work to engage them in a non-threatening conversation.

On a separate sheet of paper, answer the following questions. When the time and mood are right, ask your spouse to do the same. (This is just a sample of some of the questions on our list. Make your list more personal by adding some of your own questions.)

• What are three of your favorite restaurants?

- What is your least favorite?
- What are your favorite types of dates?
- What is your least favorite?
- What is your favorite type of movie to rent or see at the theatre?
- What is your least favorite?

After you and your spouse answer the questions, exchange lists and put them away where you can look at them when you want to do something nice for each other down the road.

7. *Avoid taking a poll before reconciling.* Over the years, we have watched God work in unique ways in each of the couples and individuals we've ministered to. One thing is for sure: God never uses the exact same methods with everyone. In our own reconciliation, if I (Michelle) had taken a poll among my family, friends, or advice circle before moving back with Joe, we never would have been able to reconcile.

When God made it clear that it was time for us to move back in together, things happened very quickly. In one day, the Holy Spirit revealed to my heart that it was time to reconcile with Joe. Although we didn't actually move back together for a couple of weeks, I started telling people about our reconciliation. Not surprisingly, most people I told were skeptical—even many Christians. Because we had been separated for so long, people expected us to date longer and attend couples counseling before actually moving back together. Not that couples counseling wouldn't have helped, but in our case that's not how God worked.

I had been going to a Christian counselor off and on for the entire two years that we were separated. I didn't go every week, but when I did go, it was always because of some problem Joe and I were trying to work through. When I called my counselor to say that we were reconciling, he begged me to wait. "Michelle, you and Joe are moving too fast. With everything you've been through together, there's no way this reconciliation will last unless you prepare better." This man knew me well, and I believe he had my best interests at heart, but the Holy Spirit was telling me otherwise.

Our son, Mick, was seven at the time we reconciled. He was ecstatic that we were going to be a family again. Jason, Joe's son from his first marriage, was in his early 20s and he was also very happy for us. But when I told my three daughters about my decision, they were all concerned and upset with me.

One was crying and said, "Mother, how can you even think about doing this? You aren't being realistic at all!" Another hung up on me when I told her. And my other daughter reminded me of all the sadness I'd gone through and was concerned that I was, once again, setting myself up for more sorrow. It took several months for my daughters to experience their own reconciliation with Joe and to accept the fact that God had indeed paved the way for us to move back together when we did.

∽◈∾

In the Bible, the apostle Paul cared about one thing: preaching the gospel of Christ to everyone—Jews and Gentiles alike. Most of the time, Paul's companions agreed with his decisions, but sometimes they didn't. One time in particular, all of Paul's Christian friends, including his traveling companion and author of the book of Acts, thought he was making a grave mistake by returning to Jerusalem because the word was out that Paul would be captured and killed:

> "This is what the Holy Spirit says: 'In this way the Jews at
> Jerusalem will bind the man who owns this belt and deliver him
> into the hands of the Gentiles.' When we had heard this, we as well
> as the local residents began begging him not to go up to Jerusalem.
>
> "Then Paul answered, 'What are you doing, weeping and

breaking my heart? For I am ready not only to be bound, but even to die at Jerusalem for the name of the Lord Jesus.' And since he would not be persuaded, we fell silent, remarking, 'The will of the Lord be done!' " (Acts 21:11-14 NASB)

If the apostle Paul had taken a poll from his "advice circle" before obeying what the Holy Spirit had instructed him to do, he might have delayed his capture, but he would have missed being used by God to deliver an important message to the Jews—and we wouldn't have his powerful message to read today (see Acts 22). There's no doubt that Paul heard the words "Well done" from God when he did finally die for the sake of the gospel several years later.

Obviously, we aren't implying that you should disregard the advice of those you have put in position to offer it. We also know that your family and close friends will sometimes be the only ones who know you and love you well enough to speak necessary truth to you. But when you are following the Lord, reading His Word, and listening for the Holy Spirit's leading, sometimes you will have to make decisions with which everyone around you will disagree. As long as your decision doesn't go directly against the Word of God, proceed with caution. If you are wrong, the Holy Spirit will stop you.

Tools that Help when Receiving Godly Counsel

Many couples and individuals who remained focused on God and content, even in the midst of their marriage crises, say they learned how to be discerning when receiving counsel. Along with our tools, we have included some of their advice as well.

1. Record and clarify the advice you receive. When you write something down, it tends to make more sense than if you mull it over in your mind. That's one reason why keeping a journal is so helpful. Our thoughts can wander all over the place, but writing forces us to put our thoughts in sensible order. One woman that I (Michelle) mentored through her marriage crisis always took notes during our weekly time together. She said it was the only way to keep her mind from being cluttered with all the other things she was trying to sort out concerning her crisis marriage. Her habit of keeping such detailed notes helped me too. Even though I like to jot down little reminders when I'm meeting with someone, her notes were much more detailed and written in her own words. We used them as a starting place for our time together each week.

Along with writing down advice, make sure to ask for clarification. Sometimes you will receive advice which makes a lot of sense at the time, but later when you try to apply it, the advice doesn't work. It may be that you have misunderstood the advice, even though you wrote it down.

2. Pray and fast if you are confused. If you begin to feel confused or backed into a corner after receiving counsel, don't make any decisions at all. Be still and wait for clear direction from God (see Psalm 46:10). Sometimes skipping a meal or two and just focusing on God's Word and asking for guidance is all it takes to get clear direction when you are feeling confused. It may be you are trying to move in a direction God doesn't want you to go and, therefore, the Holy Spirit isn't giving you peace. God is not the author of confusion (1 Corinthians 14:33), and you shouldn't make important decisions when you are feeling confused.

3. Seek confirmation from at least one other source. Sometimes the only confirmation you will have that the advice you are about to follow is truly and definitely God's will is the Bible itself. That's enough in most cases, but that shouldn't be your only source. One woman shared with us that she had used one verse in the Bible to explain to a godly man in her church why she was not free to date him, even though she desired to, after her husband had died. She was relieved when the man encouraged her to seek counsel from their pastor, and she discovered she was actually free to date and even remarry. The way in which she had interpreted the scripture wasn't accurate and she needed the help of her pastor to understand and apply what she had read.

God uses His Word, the Holy Spirit, and other believers to confirm godly advice. Sometimes, all three will be in agreement and sometimes only two. If the advice you are about to take is confirmed by only one of these sources, be patient and ask God to bring one more reliable source.

4. Be willing to put other obligations on hold—even church activities. I (Joe) will sometimes talk to a guy who wants advice on how to get support for his crisis marriage. If he tells me that he can't attend a class because of prior commitments, this concerns me. I always ask, "What is the priority in your life? Are you trying to save your marriage or aren't you? If you need to rearrange your work schedule or change your other obligations to get the help you need right now, then do it." It surprises me how many of them never do. Those who make the effort to rearrange their lives for a few weeks learn that reprioritizing what's important pays off. Most of the men admit the hassle of changing their schedules was well worth it and many credit this for saving their marriages.

※

I (Michelle) have several women each semester who come from different churches in order to attend one of our classes for marriages in crisis. In many cases, attending the classes requires them to put other commitments such as Bible studies or church activities on hold. Like Joe, I'm concerned when a woman calls to tell me her husband has just moved out, yet she refuses to rearrange her schedule to attend a class or counseling session. Recently I spoke with a young mom who had a six-month-old baby. She was at her wits' end because she and her husband had no time together and the baby was keeping her up all night. When I asked if she had a support system, she said no. When I suggested she get involved in a mom's group to help create the support she needed and start attending a class that could give her and her husband tools to strengthen their marriage—which also provided free child care—she said she would try. I knew from the sound of her voice that she probably wouldn't take my advice, and so far, she hasn't.

It takes effort to rearrange schedules and put obligations on hold in order to create the kind of advice circle you need when your marriage and family are in crisis. But if you don't make saving your marriage a priority, you will be left to make decisions on your own.

GROUP OR SUPPORT-PARTNER DISCUSSION QUESTIONS

1. *Discuss what to avoid when seeking a healthy marriage.*
2. *Discuss the tools that help when receiving godly counsel. Do you have anything else to add to the list?*
3. *Have you ever received "godly" counsel, only to find out that it wasn't godly after all?*
4. *Based on the tools in this chapter, what is the best way to set up a healthy "advice circle," and why do you think not doing so could cause (more) problems in your marriage?*
5. *Look up and discuss Romans 12:15-16.*
6. *Share anything that you are grateful for this week.*
7. *Share at least one thing that you need prayer for.*

11

Battle Outside Opposition

I am no longer in the world; and yet they themselves are
in the world, and I come to You. Holy Father, keep them
in Your name, the name which You have given Me, that
they may be one even as We are.

—JOHN 17:11, NASB

A couple of years after Michelle and I reconciled and started
serving in ministry together, a missionary pastor said
something that caused me to view marital problems in a whole new
light. He said the husbands and wives who serve God in developing
countries have a sense of unity that many Christian couples in the
United States do not have. The pastor said, "These couples face so
much outside opposition because of the severe conditions they live in
that they can't afford to turn on each other, and they understand that
as long as they remain united they can endure whatever troubles they
may face." His words made me think about the importance of a husband and wife putting up a united front, fighting their *real* enemy—
Satan—instead of warring against each other. Many times Michelle
and I argued over outside problems instead of joining forces to fight
the opposition together and going to God as a couple.

The habit of going to others for help instead of going to God first started when our marriage was in crisis. We relied on our friends and family members to give us advice for our marriage, so it stood to reason that after we reconciled we would continue to seek their advice when new troubles arose. The problem was that most of our family members and friends were more concerned with our happiness than anything else, so the advice they gave us wasn't always the best, nor was it in alignment with God's Word. Here are a few of the comments we heard from well-meaning family and friends when we were separated:

- "Do what you want to do. You deserve to be happy."
- "Hey, I know you're still legally married, but you should be enjoying life. I have this friend . . ."
- "Why are you waiting? You may as well file for divorce and move on with your life so you can be happy."
- "You know, God wants you to be happy more than anything else, and so do I. As long as you're happy, I support any decision you make."

Many of the couples and individuals we know whose marriages are in crisis have heard similar comments. It's normal for family members and friends to want you to be happy, but it's a misconception that they know you best, and, consequently, know what's best for you. The truth is God knows you best because He made you; your spouse should know you better than anyone else on earth because as husband and wife you have become "one flesh" (see Genesis 2:24). Since God knows what is best for you, even if your spouse is unwilling to work on your marriage, God can still work through him or her to accomplish His will for your life.

God's will sometimes involves suffering, and since many of our family members and friends don't want to see us suffer, this can distort their judgment. But what if God wants to grow you (and your spouse) into a deeper relationship with Him through the crises in your life?

On the cover of his book *Sacred Marriage,* Gary Thomas asks the question we must all consider: "What if God designed marriage to make us holy more than to make us happy?"[1]

〜◎〜

One of the biggest mistakes I (Michelle) made in our marriage—even after we reconciled—was to discuss problems with family members and friends before discussing them with Joe. At times I would even act on their advice without involving Joe at all, especially if the advice helped bring me happiness or relief (such as borrowing the money from my grandfather when I thought our checking account was overdrawn). By the time I would talk with Joe, his input or advice became muddled with everyone else's, often causing arguments. Before long the *outside* problem, which had nothing to do with the issue Joe or I had, was suddenly inside our home and marriage. Several times I allowed my parents' or friends' opinions to override what Joe thought was best for our family. These included what type of home or car to buy, decisions that affected our children, medical decisions, and so on. Each time I looked to others for advice before going to Joe, it caused a breakdown in communication and divided us. It also brought family and friends into our personal business and complicated the situation if I chose to ignore their advice or had to explain the outcome of a problem to them.

When Joe came home and shared his insights regarding the missionary pastor's comments, we had a long conversation that evening about changing the way we handled problems outside our marriage. That night we realized most of our marriage problems in the past could be traced to outside opposition that escalated out of control and usually involved too many opinions from family and friends wanting to "help." We realized that by going outside our marriage to discuss problems with others, we gave Satan exactly what he wanted: a husband

and wife turned against each other instead of joined with God to fight the problem as a united front.

The list below identifies some of the most common outside problems we and other couples have experienced. Each problem can be an individual issue, separate from the husband and wife relationship, and has the potential to encourage outside advice or family and friend involvement, whether you ask for it or not. Use the scale to rate the outside oppositions you may be facing right now (1=normal frustration, but not ongoing; 2=stressful, needs to be confronted; 3=crisis-level, may need professional help to resolve the problem).

As you rate your outside opposition, we want to remind you the problems we are referring to in this chapter do *not* include you and your spouse's war against each other, only trouble that comes from outside of your relationship that Satan can use to turn you *against* one another.

_____ In-law problems (either side and/or previous marriage)

_____ Conflicts with stepchildren

_____ Conflicts with biological children

_____ Problems with ex-spouses

_____ Employment-related problems

_____ Financial problems

_____ Legal problems

_____ Problems with current living conditions

_____ Injustice toward you or your spouse

_____ Death of a loved one or close friend

_____ Health problems

_____ Conflicts or misunderstandings with family or friends

_____ Problems with authorities or government

When a marriage is in crisis or has just come through a crisis, the potential for separation or divorce is extremely high when outside opposition is rated 2 or 3 in any of these areas. It's important that you have the right perspective when outside opposition comes. The sooner you and your spouse unite as a team with an "us and God against the world" mentality—even when seeking professional advice—the quicker you will solve the problem with little or no damage to your marriage.

The tools in this chapter are presented as "Battle Strategies." Although *they will work even if your spouse is not willing to participate*, these strategies will work best if your relationship fits into one of the following categories:

- You and your spouse are a "couple" and are willing to face your problems as a team.
- You and your spouse have just reconciled and want to be proactive against potential problems, or you realize outside opposition is causing tension once again.
- You and your spouse are in crisis, but are willing to try at least some of the tools in this book and/or chapter as a couple.
- You and your spouse are considering reconciliation and are willing to communicate openly about what has gone wrong in the past.

Don't lose heart if you are completing this exercise without your spouse. Keep in mind that Satan wants to use outside attacks as a means to pit you and your spouse against each other, but God wants you to view the attack as an opportunity to trust Him. Even if your spouse isn't by your side right now, you never know what God is doing behind the scenes. God may be calling you to fight the battle without your spouse's help right now. You are in a fight for your marriage and family, and Satan wants you to feel hopeless if your spouse isn't uniting with you. Listen to Paul's words to the Corinthians:

> I would like you to be free from concern. An unmarried man is concerned about the Lord's affairs—how he can please the Lord. But a married man is concerned about the affairs of this world—

how he can please his wife—and his interests are divided. An unmarried woman or virgin is concerned about the Lord's affairs: Her aim is to be devoted to the Lord in both body and spirit. But a married woman is concerned about the affairs of this world— how she can please her husband. I am saying this for your own good, not to restrict you, but that you may live in a right way in undivided devotion to the Lord. (1 Corinthians 7:32-35)

Ten Battle Strategies for Fighting Outside Opposition

1. Build a "frontline spiritual prayer team." When Michelle and I sold our business to enter into full-time ministry in 1999, she asked a small group of women to serve as our ministry prayer team. All four of these women are prayer warriors and truly care that we are in God's will, even if we aren't necessarily happy. They have committed to pray for us regularly. If we e-mail an urgent prayer request, they pray for God's will—not ours—in whatever situation we are facing.

As you can imagine, we have faced a lot of challenges over the years. We could have asked people who know us well to be on this prayer team. They would pray for our wants and desires and/or try to fix our problems. However, we knew that wasn't what we needed. We knew Satan would not want us to be in ministry, and he would do whatever he could to take us out. But with the power of intercessory prayer from people who were more concerned with what God wanted rather than what we wanted, we felt safe.

In the same way, when you assemble your spiritual team, do so with the mind-set that team members need to pray for God's will for you when outside troubles come. Unlike your support system/partner, this small prayer team does not need to know everything that is going on in your marriage. In fact, not knowing all the details is sometimes better.

Oswald Chambers writes: "If you know too much, more than God has engineered for you to know, you cannot pray. The condition of the people is so crushing that you cannot get through to reality."[1] It's not that your team *can't* know you well. But in many cases, those who are too close often get in the way of what God is trying to teach us in the midst of painful times, because they don't want us to suffer.

The job of your spiritual prayer team is to take your situation—not your requests—to God and intercede for His will in your life and marriage on your behalf. This is a powerful concept and it puts prayer on the frontlines of your battle.

2. Join forces with your spouse. If you are living with your spouse and the two of you are willing to work on your marriage together, this strategy can be fun. Of course, it will be more challenging if you and your spouse have been at odds with each other. Even so, since this exercise is about putting together a battle plan to fight against *outside* opposition rather than each other, try to convey to your spouse the concept of being a united front. Here are some ways you might word your request:

- "I know we have been fighting a lot, but it has occurred to me that we have an enemy who wants to destroy our marriage and family, and it's not you or me. Would you be willing to give our marriage another chance?"

- "I have come to realize that we are in a battle in our marriage and the real enemy is not you—it's Satan. I am going to put down my weapons against you and pick up spiritual weapons to fight for our marriage. Would you consider joining forces with me to save our marriage and family?"

- "There is an enemy who wants our marriage to end in divorce. He is after our children, and I don't want him to win. Would you join forces with me to save our children and our marriage?"

Questions like these will help place the focus where it needs to be: on the Enemy, not your spouse. We know several couples who were once in crisis and now have strong marriages as a result of learning to view the trials and tribulations in life as outside attacks on their marriages and families. They worked together as a team to overcome those problems.

If your spouse refuses to join you, before you end the conversation say something like, "If you change your mind, please let me know. We would make a powerful team." Remember to stay calm and not react to the Enemy's tactics to divide your family. Your friends and family may love you dearly, but there is no other team on earth more powerful than a husband and wife who are focused on God. Don't negate godly counsel and support, but do your best to be united with your spouse first.

3. Join forces with your powerful God. Our pastor often reminds us that life is a series of storms. He says, "You are either just coming out of a storm, are in one now, or will be in one shortly." He also encourages us to not lose heart in the midst of a storm: "God is more concerned about your character than your comfort. The best thing you can do in your storm is to surrender all to Him."

When you lock arms with the God of this universe (with or without your spouse), any battle you fight on this earth will be won. Remember that the strategy of the Devil is to divide us and take our joy away so we can't witness to others effectively. Your responsibility as a believer is to be self-controlled so that you can have peace and joy in the midst of your tribulation. If you are fighting a battle without your spouse, the key is to stay focused on the problem and never view your spouse as the enemy.

4. Discuss the attack and stand firm. How can you say you trust God if you don't go to Him *first* when attacks come? Likewise, how can you expect your spouse to feel like your partner and best friend if you refuse to discuss outside attacks with him or her first, or at all? Your spouse needs to be the first person you go to (after God, of course) when a problem occurs because he or she will be your best ally. God will equip you as a couple with the supernatural power of His Holy Spirit. Even if your spouse refuses to join forces with you at this time, keep trusting God and practicing these strategies. Your self-control and perseverance will be attractive to your spouse, and you will have the mindset of partnering against the troubles of this world when and if your spouse repents.

The next part of this exercise is to stand firm. So often, we run in the face of conflict or trouble, but that isn't what God says to do. We are to flee from sin (see 1 Timothy 6:11), but God says to stand firm against Satan: "Put on the full armor of God so that you can take your stand against the devil's schemes" (Ephesians 6:11).

Practically speaking, imagine you received a letter telling you your driver's license is going to be suspended. You are upset because you know the DMV has made a mistake. You are also frustrated because you will have to take time off work the next day to resolve the problem. Instead of discussing the problem with your spouse, you choose to keep the mix-up to yourself.

Even though your problem has nothing to do with your spouse, you might be more uptight than usual that evening, and as a result, not as loving. The next day you take care of the problem. When you get home, you decide to discuss it with your spouse. But instead of your spouse understanding, he or she responds in a sarcastic tone of voice and says, "Oh, now I know why you were behaving so strangely last night. Why didn't you just tell me you were upset about that letter instead of being so rude all evening?" Your spouse's response triggers old mental tapes that begin to replay in your mind. Soon you are both dragging things up from the past and accusing each other of "never changing." Maybe the argument escalates to the point where you or your spouse walks out the door and makes a rash decision that will cause major consequences. That's what Satan hopes will happen.

The Enemy uses small problems to cause division in marriages all the time. When we keep daily frustrations from each other, the potential for sharing them with people outside the marriage is higher. Most couples and individuals we know whose marriages are in crisis because of third-party involvement admit they had stopped including their spouses in the everyday events and outside problems in their lives. Some say it was because they didn't want to hear their spouse's advice or negative comments. Even so, real communication means talking about things that are not always pleasant. It takes work, but it's worth the effort because good communication protects the marriage relationship.

5. Enter into battle with a clean and sober mind. No one likes to suffer, but when one or both spouses turn to alcohol, drugs, shopping, or overeating in an effort to numb pain, they will only prolong the suffering. Paul tells us in Romans that all believers will suffer until we leave this world and join Christ in eternal life. The only way to grow through our troubles is to face them sober. Kris is an example of a woman who realized the effect alcohol was taking on her family and made the decision to live life sober.

"I started having a glass of wine every night when I came home from work just so I could relax. By the time I realized it had become a problem, I was drinking several glasses every night. One reason I kept drinking was because it created an atmosphere that was calm and peaceful in my home. My ex-husband and I didn't fight when he came over or called, and the kids didn't get on my nerves. I just got a little buzz going as soon as I hit the door, and everything else seemed like no big deal.

"But one day I realized that even though things were 'peaceful' at home, none of us were communicating, and I wasn't taking responsibility for some outside problems going on in my life. I had gotten used to pretending things were great when in fact they weren't. I was also shirking my parenting responsibilities with my two children who were just hitting adolescence. As long as I worked in a fun atmosphere during the day, sipped wine, and listened to some great jazz in the evening, life was good."

Kris gave up her addiction a year ago and began dealing with some tough challenges in her life. She has since turned her life toward God and continues to grow closer to Him daily, in spite of some painful trials. "I've decided I would rather be sober and deal with reality, even if it's painful at times, than live in a pretend world and miss life altogether."

6. Stay connected to each other in the midst of trials. Some problems are over soon after they begin. However, other problems may take days, weeks, or even years to resolve. Several years ago Michelle and I interviewed eight couples who had strong marriages in spite of serious outside opposition in their lives. We used their stories to create an eight-week class titled, "Riding the Waves of Tribulation in Your Marriage—God's Way." One thing we noticed when compiling the information from these couples was that they stayed closely connected to each other during their troubles. Here are a few of the tribulations these couples faced: the death of a child (one couple even lost two children); the challenges of parenting disabled children; financial loss; living next to dangerous, gun-toting neighbors; and getting married knowing the husband would be in a wheelchair within 10 years.

Each couple had their own unique story concerning how they survived their storm and grew closer to God and each other in the midst of it. But the common thread they all shared was their ability to stay connected to each other and face their challenges with a team spirit. It would have been so easy for these couples to blame each other, but in each case they chose to put up a united front, and their marriages still stand strong to this day.

It's important to remember that men and women often view problems from drastically different perspectives. The Holy Spirit is the key to helping you view your problems, not from your perspective or your spouse's, but from God's perspective. Remember that the differences in your temperaments (discussed in chapter 5) will also cause you to view problems differently. To complicate matters, what you may perceive as a problem may be something that your spouse doesn't even struggle with. Nothing puts a stop to sharing our problems with each other more than a response such as, "What's the big deal? I don't see that as a problem." Carl and Peggy are an example of a couple who views outside problems from different perspectives.

Carl and Peggy both had careers in education when they met and married. At each report-card period, Carl would labor and fret for days about his upcoming parent-teacher conferences and dreaded the thought of back-to-back meetings with parents, some of whom might be upset with the lack of progress their child was making. On the other hand, Peggy didn't see those conferences as problematic at all. "Honey, why are you getting so worked up about this? I have twice as many conferences as you do and you don't see me getting all uptight about it."

What Peggy failed to understand was that while she was invigorated by the challenging interactions and conversations that were a part of parent-teacher conferences (and actually welcomed them into her schedule as a nice break from teaching), those very same types of conferences literally drained Carl emotionally and physically. This couple had to learn to accept each others' different temperaments and preferences before they could learn how to become united when outside problems threatened their marriage.

If your spouse is willing, set aside weekly time to discuss whatever outside problems you may be facing. Do your part to listen and ask questions, and let your spouse share how he or she views the problem(s). Ask for advice, and then let your spouse know you will take his or her advice to heart. Do your best to create an atmosphere of safety and intimacy for your spouse.

～❦～

It is good to remember that women need to talk and connect emotionally, and men like to sleep and connect sexually when stress and conflicts occur. Many women have told me (Michelle) that just making changes in their schedules in order to have the energy and time to connect sexually with their husbands at least twice a week changed their marriages from crisis-filled to joy-filled. In most cases their husbands not only dealt with outside problems quicker, but had a much better attitude and a desire to talk and connect emotionally!

Joe and I are convinced that Satan has caused more division between husbands and wives in the area of sexual intimacy than any other area. It's not only women who get too busy for sexual intimacy; there are plenty of men who sexually neglect their wives. Satan knows that God supernaturally designed sex to physically, emotionally, and spiritually connect a man and woman. If he can get married couples to disconnect sexually, it will cause pent-up frustration as well as open the door to marital unfaithfulness. Oftentimes sexual problems have little to do with each other and more to do with outside problems such as a physical condition, illness, or stress. If you and your spouse are struggling in the area of sexual intimacy, take the time to discuss it openly with each other and with a counselor or health-care professional, if necessary.

7. Be physically fit for battle. Several years ago I (Michelle) lost my dad, Vito, to cancer. Even though my parents were divorced when I was three years old, I was close to my dad; his illness and death took a toll on me. During the three-month period while my dad's cancer worsened, I was aware that eating right and getting enough rest would be even more important than usual. Joe and I paid careful attention not to overbook ourselves, and we took a break from teaching classes. Even though there was a lot of related outside opposition during my dad's illness and death, there was a sense of peace, and Joe and I came through the stressful time as a team.

However, a few years later when Joe's mom, Marge, died of cancer, it was a different story. Instead of being proactive about taking good care of ourselves as we did when my dad was diagnosed, we continued to run busy schedules, neglect our health, and get little sleep. Not only did we continue teaching classes, but we agreed to spearhead a huge community marriage seminar. (His mom passed away five weeks prior to the event.) Throughout her illness, Joe and I were traveling back and forth six hours one way in order to visit her and help her make medical decisions. After she died there were other decisions to be made. Even though Joe's older brother was taking care of the majority of those decisions, we were still both exhausted by the time everything was over.

A few days later an outside attack blindsided us. Because we weren't prepared when the problem hit, our first instinct was to turn on each other. Our particular problem had to do with a family member, and we viewed the opposition from two opposing points of view. But since we understood the importance of uniting in the face of outside opposition, we faced the problem as a couple and made an appointment to discuss the situation with someone we knew and trusted. As a result, we were able to resolve the issue quickly without damage to our relationship. Since then, we have been extremely proactive concerning our health any time we are dealing with outside problems.

8. *Wait for the "General's" orders.* A couple of years after we reconciled and soon after our commitment to put up a united front, one of our children was in crisis. We were faced with making an important decision that would have lasting effects. I (Michelle) would have nor-

mally gone to family members before discussing the problem with Joe since it involved my daughter Heather. This time, however, I asked Joe first, but his answer wasn't one I wanted to hear: "Since we still have a while before we have to make a final decision, let's wait and see what happens." *See what happens?* I thought. I didn't want to wait; I wanted to act quickly. But since we were working on being united, I tried to be patient.

A month later, which to me seemed more like a year, I was scheduled to attend a women's retreat. I was tempted to get everyone's advice about our situation at the retreat, but I wanted to honor God by doing what Joe and I had agreed to do. The second morning of the retreat, I grabbed my Bible and journal and took a walk. Sitting beside a river, I wrote my problem to God and searched the Bible for an answer that I could use to convince Joe to make our decision now, rather than continue waiting. I did find an answer, but not the one I was looking for: "Be still, and know that I am God" (Psalm 46:10). I had never noticed that verse before, but that day it became one of the most important verses in the Bible to me.

Those who knew me before that weekend retreat will tell you that waiting and being still were not in my nature. I came back from that retreat with a new perspective, and I told Joe I would no longer rush decisions we faced. It was the good thing too, because the particular situation we were facing with Heather took another year, almost to the day, to get an answer. As I waited during that year, God used the time to prove He was in control of every outside problem we had or ever will have. Trusting God (and Joe) wasn't easy at first, but the longer I waited, the easier it became.

One year later we took custody of our ten-month-old granddaughter, Krissy, and she lived with us for almost three years. Our waiting period allowed certain important circumstances to play out in a way that we now understand.

Our daughter Heather had been on drugs since she was a teenager. She was in her early 20s, living on the streets when Krissy was born. At first we thought Heather would get off drugs in order to raise Krissy, but she went right back to the streets when Krissy was only a few hours old. When the social worker from the hospital contacted us, we were told that we had six months to make a decision as to whether or not to take legal custody. Joe believed that if we rushed to take custody, it would not give Heather any incentive to get off drugs. It was during this "waiting" period that God gave me Psalm 46:10. Three months later Heather did get off drugs and checked herself into a rehab center. In the months that followed, we were relieved to know God had answered our prayers by getting Heather off drugs. But a couple of months later she returned to her destructive lifestyle. Again we waited and prayed. This time God gave us His answer quickly, and we took custody of Krissy within two weeks.

Looking back, I can see how the Enemy could have used this problem to divide Joe and me again. Most of our family and friends expressed opposing opinions (even though we weren't even asking) while we waited for God's answer. One family member asked, "How will you go skiing on the weekends if you have a toddler?" Another said, "Why did you wait so long? I thought you should have taken her when she was first born!" If I had listened to all their advice and argued with Joe about what was best for us, our granddaughter would have been the one to suffer. Instead, we stayed united. When Heather turned her life around a couple of years later, we knew how to wait and trust God during the unification process of Heather and Krissy. The day we went to court in San Francisco, California, to release custody of Krissy back to Heather, the judge said, "This is a joyful day for me. It's not often that I get the privilege of seeing a mother with Heather's background take custody of her child." There were tears in the courtroom that day, and we knew God had done a miraculous thing.

Today Heather and Krissy have a wonderful relationship with each other and with God, and we all thank Him for a beautiful ending to a situation that appeared hopeless for years and could have divided the whole family forever.

9. *Face your battle with the right attitude.* When self-control is coupled with the power of the Holy Spirit, any problem can be used for good: "And we know that in all things God works for the good of those who love him, who have been called according to his purpose" (Romans 8:28). It may be difficult to sing praises and be thankful when we are facing trials, but the couples who have learned to view problems as an opportunity to draw closer to God and to each other have strong marriages and make powerful teams. Kelli learned this principle just in time.

Kelli had been asking God to do something about her unhappy life. "I just wasn't happy anymore, and I blamed my marriage as the reason for my unhappiness. I expected James to give more of himself to me and our marriage, but he seemed so self-centered all the time. When I would tell him how unhappy I was, he would just shrug his shoulders and walk away."

Kelli prayed for direction, but God seemed to be silent. Finally, feeling hopeless, she decided to leave James, thinking a separation might shake him up and cause him to treat her better. As she was making plans to walk out on her marriage, she was hit with an unexpected outside problem: She was fired from her job.

"I was shocked. I had worked there almost 15 years, and the last thing I expected was to get fired. Then the reality of what I was facing hit me. I was trapped. How could I move out without having a job to support myself? When I told James I had been fired, his response wasn't at all what I expected. Instead of being angry or even upset, he put his arms around me and showed me more love and concern than I had gotten from him in years!

"At a time when I felt the whole world was against me—James was right there! What is even more amazing is that since I've been home and not working, I've realized it wasn't my marriage I was unhappy with after all—it was my job. God answered my prayer, but since it came in the form of a "problem," I almost missed it! I've decided that from now on, I'm going to praise God when a problem occurs. It might just be His answer to something I've been praying about!"

The next time an outside problem occurs, praise God. Trust Him to work out all things for your best interest.

10. Celebrate victories and defeats with your spouse. One thing Michelle and I like to do after we navigate through an attack, or sometimes even in the midst of it, is to celebrate. Years ago I learned the power of celebrating in the midst of trouble. A company I worked for in a local mall closed down. I went into work one day to find out I was out of a job. It was pretty shocking at first and I wasn't happy about it, but I got the idea of buying a box of candy and celebrating the job loss as a "job change" instead. I called Michelle and told her what happened; she came to the mall expecting me to be upset. She was surprised to find me playing the piano at a music store and handing out chocolates to customers. When she asked what I was doing, I told her I decided to celebrate our problem rather than worry about it. I had asked the store owner if I could play one of his pianos to relieve some stress. My choice to celebrate helped both of us view the problem with a better attitude. The best part was that the music store owner was so impressed with how I handled the job loss that he offered me an interim job selling pianos!

Every time we have experienced outside attacks since then, we either go out to dinner or just take some time off together to go somewhere special. Celebrating helps create a light at the end of the tunnel for both of us. I often remind guys that marriage should be fun, and they need to spend time with their wives just celebrating life.

What better time to celebrate than after or during an attack that Satan wants to use to take away our joy and divide our marriages? For God says, "Rejoice always; pray without ceasing; in everything give thanks; for this is God's will for you in Christ Jesus" (1 Thessalonians 5:16-18 NASB).

∞

If you have been practicing the exercises and implementing the tools in this book with your spouse, you are on your way to having a marriage that will last. But even if your spouse has not participated, it is still possible to reconcile. In the last chapter we will help you to go forth with confidence, regardless of the outcome of your marriage.

GROUP OR SUPPORT-PARTNER DISCUSSION QUESTIONS

1. *Discuss any "outside" opposition that you and your spouse are facing right now.*
2. *Discuss the benefits of the 10 battle strategies.*
3. *Have you had an opportunity to practice any of the tools in this book with your spouse? If so, which ones were especially helpful? If not, have you tried?*
4. *On a scale of one to five, with five being highest, what was the depth of your relationship with the Lord at the beginning of this book? What is it now? What about with your spouse?*
5. *Look up and discuss Romans 13:8-14.*
6. *What are you grateful for this week?*
7. *How can your support partner or small group pray for you and your spouse as a couple in order to fight any outside opposition you are facing?*

12

Reconciling—God's Way

*R*ecently we attended a 50th wedding anniversary. When we asked Manuel and Mona what advice they would give to young married couples today, they answered, "We would tell them to stay committed to each other and spend time together. We married young and had no money for the first several years. But we enjoyed our children, and we always faced our problems together as a couple." Mona smiled and added, "I would also tell couples not to make such a big deal out of everything and to have a sense of humor!"

If your dreams of celebrating 50 or more years of marriage have been dashed because of an unwanted divorce, or if your marriage is in crisis and you wonder if you will even see your next anniversary, we understand. We wish we could take your hand and pray with you right now, but we are with you in spirit and have prayed for you often while writing this book. While we may never personally meet you, God knew you would be reading these words and He knows the outcome of your marriage. However, although He wants your marriage to be saved and for you to enjoy many years of happily wedded bliss, it is not His number one desire for you. The truth is that above all else He wants you to be one with Him. In *My Utmost for His Highest*, Oswald Chambers writes:

> If you are going through a solitary way, read John 17, it will explain exactly why you are where you are—Jesus has prayed that you may be one with the Father as He is. . . . He allows these

things for His own purpose. . . . When we understand what God is after we will not get mean and cynical. Jesus has prayed nothing less for us than absolute oneness with Himself as He was one with the Father. . . . God will not leave us alone until we *are* one with Him, because Jesus has prayed that we may be.[1]

The dreams you have for a happy marriage pale in comparison to the dreams God has for you if you will stay focused on Him and trust Him to work out what is best for you. As you come to the end of this book, you will have to trust God to work out your particular situation in His timing, as He did with us and the hundreds of couples we have ministered to over the years. We have asked some of the couples whose marriages were once in crisis and who now serve with us in ministry what they would say to you if they were sitting across the table from you having coffee. Here is what each couple shared.

FROM: MARK AND DEBBIE
TO: THE PERSON TRYING TO SAVE A MARRIAGE ALONE

I (Debbie) want to say that if you are working on your marriage with an unwilling spouse, you must not underestimate the power that you have with God by your side. If your spouse is in sin, you don't need to be his or her judge and jury. When I didn't want to save our marriage, Mark had to learn to get out of the way so that God could convict me of my hard heart. Learn to entrust your spouse to God and take care of your own side of the street. Your relationship with your spouse will never be as important as your relationship with God. The truth is, you are not going to heaven with your spouse by your side—you will stand before God on your own.

I (Mark) want to encourage you to pray without ceasing—it is the most powerful weapon you have! So many people forget that, and they get busy trying to play god in their spouses' lives. I had to learn to entrust Debbie to God, even when I knew she was walking outside of God's will. If you will reconcile with God first and do what He tells you to do, then when your spouse repents, you will be ready to reconcile. If your spouse never comes on board, then at least you will be able to move on knowing that you did your part.

FROM: MARION AND JEANNE
TO: THE COUPLE WHOSE MARRIAGE IS IN CRISIS

We have been married 45 years, but there was a time when we thought our marriage would end in divorce. Even though we were Christians, you would have never known it by the way we behaved toward each other. I (Jeanne) used to secretly wish I could be a "godly widow" so I wouldn't have to deal with our marital problems anymore. But God had other plans for us. Instead He wanted us to learn to take our focus off each other and put it where it belonged—on Him.

Jeanne and I (Marion) were married 10 years and served in our church when our marriage fell into crisis. Neither one of us wanted to work very hard to save the marriage, but because we were Christians we felt that we at least needed to give it a shot. We want to encourage you as a couple to learn to pray together—from your hearts. A counselor taught us how to pray as a couple, and even though in the beginning we used the prayers to give little digs to each other, God used our prayers to reveal years of unresolved issues in our hearts. We never miss a day without praying with and for each other. We are praying for you too.

FROM: CLINT AND PENNY
TO: THE COUPLE OR INDIVIDUAL WHOSE
MARRIAGE LOOKS HOPELESS

Nothing is impossible with God. We are grateful that God gave us a second chance when we remarried after being divorced for 11 years. But that wasn't just something special He reserved for our marriage. As long as your spouse has not remarried, your marriage can still be saved. No matter how hopeless things might seem, stay focused on God and let Him lead you. Apply the tools in this book and let your walk match your talk.

Think of your marriage as you would an invitation to a sacred dance with God. What is required on your part is to accept His invitation, take His hand, and let Him lead you out onto the dance floor. There you will apply the steps you've been practicing along the way. Sure, some steps will be much harder to take than others. That's to be expected. There are stumbling blocks in every relationship and there will be times it seems that for every mountaintop you dance on, a valley awaits on the other side. But remember that no matter how hampered your steps become, do not hesitate for a moment to listen to the music and follow God's lead in *whatever* process He uses to mend your marriage. Keep dancing . . . and know that we'll be dancing right beside you.

～☙～

The majority of couples who have come through our ministry over the years agree that if their marriages had not been in crisis, they would not have had as strong a relationship with God. One night in my (Joe's) men's group, one of the guys shared that he had bought each of his three sons a Bible that day. I asked him, "When was the last time you bought your boys Bibles?" He shook his head and looked down when he answered, "I'm ashamed to say never. My sons are in their late teens and if my wife hadn't left me, I wouldn't have come to this group and learned about the Lord. If there is one good thing that has come out of my marriage crisis, it's that I'm working on being the godly man I should have been all these years."

God wants us to reconcile—but He wants us to reconcile *His* way. His ways are not our ways. For instance, how often have you heard the "ball and chain" example of marriage? I heard it all the time as a young man, and even now there are jokes and advertisements that suggest that marriage is not meant to be fun. But that's man's thinking—not God's.

~⊚~

Human thinking also differs in terms of understanding God's laws. Many people complain that God's commands in the Bible are too constrictive. I (Michelle) remember the night that I told God He couldn't tell me how to live. When I walked away for 14 rebellious years, I thought I was "free," but it was just the opposite; I was enslaved to a sinful lifestyle and the consequences were far-reaching. God's laws do not constrict us. But unless we spend time in His Word and practice what He tells us to do, we will never fully learn to trust that His laws actually set us free. Something happened recently that caused me to think about how important it is for you to practice the tools in this book in order to trust that they will work in your crisis marriage.

Our sixth-grade granddaughter, Krissy, told me about a science experiment that she saw in a video at school last week. Here's how she explained it: "Mimi, you should have seen this experiment that had to do with Newton's three laws of motion! A teacher told a girl to stand in a particular spot and he was going to drop a cannonball hanging from a rope in the ceiling. He told her that the ball would swing toward her, but that she didn't need to duck because it would be impossible for the ball to hit her. The ball could swing only the same distance as the length of the rope. But every time the teacher let go of the ball, the girl ducked—she never did believe the ball wouldn't hit her, and she never trusted what the teacher said."

I told Krissy I would probably be just like that girl: "There's no way I would trust that a cannonball wasn't going to hit me if it was swinging right toward me." Krissy agreed.

The science experiment got me to thinking about what causes people to trust a proven theory. I wondered if a science teacher who understood and conducted these types of experiments would trust the ball to not hit him or her. I decided to ask our son-in-law, Joey, since he is a high school science teacher. "Joey, since you teach science and understand the physics, would you flinch and duck if a cannonball came swinging at you, even though you knew that it couldn't hit you?" Joey said that he would probably flinch the first time or two, but after that he wouldn't. He went on to explain that the pendulum experiment Krissy had seen always causes students to duck because they don't understand how the laws of motion work. As I suspected, because our son-in-law practices and teaches science, it would be easier for him to trust the experiment. But since I have never studied physics, unless I practiced daily for a long time, I would probably always duck when the ball was dropped.

In the same way that we need to physically test a scientific hypothesis before believing it will work, we must also step out in faith to "test" God's principles in order to believe they'll work. For example, if you have spent a lot of time in God's Word and have been a Christian for many years, the tools in this book will probably be fairly easy for you to grasp. With little practice, you will be able to see major changes in your life and in your marriage. On the other hand, if you are a new Christian or haven't spent time reading or studying the Bible, many of the tools we have shared may not make sense to you, since most are based on God's laws and have to do with a spiritual realm that is hard to understand. The Holy Spirit is the One who reveals truth to us as we step out in faith, believing that what God says is true.

But a natural man does not accept the things of the Spirit of God, for they are foolishness to him; and he cannot understand them, because they are spiritually appraised. But he who is spiritual appraises all things, yet he himself is appraised by no one. For who has known the mind of the Lord, that he will instruct him? But we have the mind of Christ. (1 Corinthians 2:14-16, NASB)

GO FORTH—GOD'S WAY

If you have been meeting with your spouse, support partner, or small group on a weekly basis while practicing the tools in this book, your 12 weeks are coming to a close. But that doesn't mean your weekly time has to end. As we said in chapter 2, a healthy support system is vital and should not be given up even if your crisis is over. Keep growing in your walk with Jesus and with others, regardless of what is happening in your marriage. These last tools are designed to use in whatever situation your marriage is in at the end of the book. Adjust the tools accordingly, if your situation changes.

If Your Marriage Has Gotten Worse

If your spouse has moved out and/or filed for a divorce since you started reading the book, ask your support partner and/or small group if they would be willing to go through another 12-week study. For ideas, contact your local church, a Christian bookstore, or our organization. Stay focused on God and don't forget to test any advice that you receive against God's Word.

Trust God to work out your marriage situation His way, and consider fasting and praying one day a week for your spouse. Rather than clinging to your spouse and trying to talk him or her out of leaving, let God be your number one focus. We know this isn't easy, but it is the best thing you can do and your actions will honor the Lord.

If Your Marriage Is Still in Crisis, but Has Not Gotten Worse

If things are about the same as when you first started the book, continue meeting with your support team. If you don't already attend a same-gender Bible study or small group consider joining one to work on any new issues you may have discovered while going through this book, such as addiction, unresolved childhood issues or abuse, boundary problems, and so on.

Also, if the Lord leads you to ask your spouse if he or she would be willing to go through some of the tools together now and then, do so. If your spouse declines, just keep doing your part. The most important thing you can do is to continue growing in your own walk with the Lord.

If Your Marriage Is No Longer in Crisis

If you and your spouse have reconciled, consider going through another 12-week study to strengthen your marriage. We have discovered that the first five years back together are the most vulnerable. Many of the couples, including us, were not prepared for what we experienced after reconciling. While we have discovered several tools that can help you stay committed and avoid another marriage crisis, here are seven of the most important ones:

1. *Stay connected with couples who have good marriages.* It's easy to fall into old behaviors once your marriage has been in crisis, especially if you were separated. Once you reconcile, if you spend time with couples whose marriages are healthy and who speak highly of each other, you will have fewer chances of outside problems causing a crisis

between the two of you. (Remember to guard against "coveting" that healthy marriage, as we mentioned in chapter 10.)

2. Don't get involved in helping others too soon. The typical response from a healed couple is to rush into ministry. We have found that it's best to wait one year. Many of the couples whose marriages fell into crisis again had started serving in a ministry within the first couple of months. Instead of taking time to secure their own marriage, they began "transferring" their issues and hurts to other couples. This not only hurts other couples, but weakens your ability to deal with new issues that will arise as a result of the reconciliation. Remember how difficult it was for us to admit that we were in crisis again after the pastor renewed our vows and we were trying to serve in a ministry together? Waiting one year and continuing to work on your marriage will lessen the chance of that happening to you.

3. Set aside regular times to discuss household and family matters. The couples whose marriages stayed strong after they reconciled (including ours) have learned the importance of being proactive concerning outside problems. We like to go for coffee on a Saturday or Monday morning at least once a month to discuss potential problem areas, or to make important decisions for our ministry, home, or family. One of the couples we do ministry with does something a little more creative.

Clint and Penny found it was helpful to schedule a weekend away every three months. They call this a "mini marriage retreat."[2] During their time away with God, they pray and set goals for the coming months in several different areas such as finances, spiritual growth, family relationships, physical health, and so on. Each time they take a mini marriage retreat, they review the previous quarter's goals and thank God for His direction before moving on to set goals for the coming quarter.

4. Self-nurture as a couple. Don't give up doing your own self-nurturing, but begin to implement couple activities. If you don't have a hobby to do together, pray about getting one. Add fun into your marriage by doing things that are creative and fun. We belong to a group at our church that gets together monthly just to play games, eat, and laugh together. Couples who have fun together will keep humor and laughter in their lives—which neutralizes the everyday pressures of life.

5. Review the tools in this book regularly. Couples whose marriages have remained intact for five years and longer have told us that they continue to review and use the tools that brought them back together. Even we review the tools and continually add to them. We have been happily reconciled for nearly 18 years, but we will never take our marriage for granted. We will always practice what we preach because we know that by doing so Satan will not have a chance to knock us down again.

6. Give back. After your crisis has been over for at least one year, step out in faith and volunteer to help others in some way. This is where knowing your spiritual gifts and natural temperaments can be helpful (chapter 5). You may even want to serve in a reconciliation ministry! We get calls on a regular basis from all over the United States from reconciled couples who want to help others whose marriages are in crisis. One thing is for sure: Once people have experienced a crisis in their own marriages and they are focused on God, He will allow them to use the pain from their pasts to help others!

7. Grow spiritually. The most important thing you can do to protect your marriage is to mature in your walk with the Lord. You and your spouse may like to do couples devotions, or you may enjoy doing your devotions separately. Don't force each other to do a couples devotion if that isn't comfortable, but do make certain to take care of your own spiritual growth. All the couples we know who were once in crisis but now have great marriages have learned this principle.

CLOSING WORDS

From Michelle to the Women

My hope and prayer for you is that you will learn to pray for your husband when you are frustrated with him, and try your best not to parent him. It's hard not to want to parent because as women, most of us like to nurture and keep things peaceful at home. But if you aren't careful, you can get in God's way. You must learn to step aside and trust Him to work out your marriage. Your job is to pray and always speak the truth in love. With God by your side, you will never be alone. The verse I want to leave you with is Isaiah 30:21: "Whether you turn to the right or to the left, your ears will hear a voice behind you saying, 'This is the way; walk in it.'"

From Joe to the Men

Remember that you're in a battle and you need to keep up the good fight. Stay in a men's group, always be accountable to someone, and love your wife. You may have heard it said, "Stay out of my business and I'll stay out of yours." Well, God tells us the opposite: "Get into my business and I'll take care of yours." The verse I want to leave you with is Isaiah 58:8: "Then your light will break forth like the dawn, and your healing will quickly appear; then your righteousness will go before you, and the glory of the LORD will be your rear guard."

GROUP OR SUPPORT-PARTNER DISCUSSION QUESTIONS

1. What is your current situation with your spouse?

2. Which tools have been most helpful over the past 12 weeks?

3. Which tools have been the most difficult for you to implement?

4. *What area of ministry do you feel you might like to serve in once your marriage crisis is over (regardless of the outcome)?*

5. *Discuss the concept that God cares more about your relationship with Him than He does about your marriage.*

6. *Read and discuss 1 Corinthians 1:9-10.*

7. *What is your plan now in terms of a class or support system? Close in prayer and ask God to show you the way—His way. God bless you.*

Notes

CHAPTER 2

1. Henry Cloud and John Townsend, *Safe People* (Grand Rapids, MI: Zondervan, 1995), 167.

CHAPTER 3

1. Penny A. Bragg, *The Path of Most Resistance* (Dublin, CA: Inverse Ministries, Inc., 2004), 66.
2. Ibid., 112.
3. Inverse Ministries, Inc., Clint and Penny Bragg, Dublin, California.
4. Restored Hearts Ministry, Earl and Kaye Stotler, Chico, California.
5. J. Vernon McGee, *Thru the Bible* (Nashville: Thomas Nelson Publishers, 2002), 98.
6. Creative Connections Ministry, Don and Kathy Coryell, Riverbank, California.
7. Oswald Chambers, *My Utmost for His Highest* (Grand Rapids, MI: Oswald Chambers Publications Association, Ltd., 1963), 285.
8. Gary Chapman, *Hope for the Separated,* (Chicago: Moody Press, 1996, 1982), 58-59.
9. Prodigal Sons and Daughters, Ken and Jane Meuers, Turlock, California.
10. Several choices of spiritual gifts tests are available online at no cost.

CHAPTER 4

1. Dr. Robert Ross, Ph.D., LMFT (Anchor Counseling, Lexington, KY), letter to authors
2. Marriage Alive seminars, Dave and Claudia Arp, Marriage Alive International (www.marriagealive.com, 865-690-5877).
3. Warren W. Wiersbe, *Be Real* (Colorado Springs: Cook Communications Ministries, 1972), 45.
4. Chambers, *My Utmost for His Highest,* 15.

CHAPTER 5

1. Mels Carbonell, *Uniquely You in Christ* (Blue Ridge, GA: Mels Carbonell, 1998), 1, 14.
2. Ibid., 1, 14.
3. Fred and Florence Littauer, *After Every Wedding Comes a Marriage* (Eugene, OR: Harvest House Publishers, 1997), 38.
4. Ibid., 382.
5. Gary Chapman, *The Five Love Languages* (Chicago: Northfield Publishing, 1992), 24.
6. Ibid., 156.
7. Bill and Pam Farrel, *Men Are Like Waffles—Women Are Like Spaghetti* (Eugene, OR: Harvest House, 2001), 16.
8. H. Norman Wright, *What Men Want* (Ventura, CA: Regal Books, 1996), 15-16
9. Ibid., 141.
10. Bill and Pam Farrel, *Men Are Like Waffles—Women Are Like Spaghetti* (Eugene, OR: Harvest House, 2001), 35.

CHAPTER 6

1. Gary Thomas, *Sacred Marriage* (Grand Rapids, MI: Zondervan, 2000), 162, 163.
2. Gary Chapman, *The Five Love Languages of Children* (Chicago: Northfield Publishing, 1997), 156.
3. Ibid.
4. Bill and Pam Farrel, *Men Are Like Waffles—Women Are Like Spaghetti* (Eugene, OR: Harvest House, 2001), 49.
5. Ibid.

CHAPTER 7

1. Williard F. Harley, *His Needs, Her Needs* (Grand Rapids, MI: Revell Books, 2001) 97-98.

CHAPTER 8

1. Henry Cloud and John Townsend, *Boundaries in Marriage* (Grand Rapids, MI: Zondervan, 2002), 251.
2. James Dobson, *Love Must Be Tough* (Dallas, TX: Word, 1996)
3. Henry Cloud and John Townsend, *Safe People* (Grand Rapids, MI: Zondervan, 1995), 96.
4. Karen Kayser, *When Love Dies: The Process of Marital Dissatisfaction* (New York: The Guilford Press, 1993), pp. 93-96, adapted.
5. H. Norman Wright, *What Men Want* (Ventura, CA: Regal Books, 1996), 45-46.

6. Dr. David Hawkins, *Nine Critical Mistakes Most Couples Make* (Eugene, OR: Harvest House, 2005), 178.
7. Facts on Domestic Violence, www.endabuse.org/resources/facts/DomesticViolence.pdf.

Chapter 9

1. Ed Wheat, M.D., *How to Save Your Marriage Alone* (Grand Rapids, MI: Zondervan, 1983).

Chapter 10

1. Gary Chapman, *Hope for the Separated* (Chicago: Moody Press, 1992), 68.

Chapter 11

1. Gary Thomas, *Sacred Marriage* (Grand Rapids, MI: Zondervan, 2000), cover.

Chapter 12

1. Oswald Chambers, *My Utmost for His Highest* (May 22).
2. Clint and Penny Bragg, *Discovering God's Vision for Your Marriage Workbook* (Dublin, CA: Inverse Ministries, Inc.), 46.

About the Authors

Joe and Michelle Williams are the founders and directors of the International Center for Reconciling God's Way—a faith-based, non-profit organization providing help and hope for marriages in crisis. With divorce in their backgrounds prior to becoming Christians, and a two-year separation in their own marriage, as Christians, they can relate to most couples whose marriages are in crisis. They have served in ministry since 1990 and in 1997 they coauthored a workbook and support-partner handbook.

Through speaking at national marriage conferences and providing workshops for pastors and leaders of all denominations, Joe and Michelle have been instrumental in helping churches begin marriage reconciliation ministries. They co-host a radio program with other couples in their community called "Communicating God's Way," as well as teach classes to individuals and couples who want to reconcile their marriages. Both Joe and Michelle have received bachelor of Christian counseling degrees from Scofield Graduate School and Seminary in Modesto, California.

Joe and Michelle married in 1982 and have five children—his, hers, and a son of their own born in 1983—and ten grandchildren. They reside in Modesto where Joe serves as pastor of discipleship and Michelle as assistant director of discipleship and director of women's ministry in their local church. For more information contact:

The International Center for Reconciling God's Way, Inc.

PO Box 1543, Modesto, CA 95353

209-578-HELP (4357) or 1-800-205-6808

www.reconcilinggodsway.org

E-mail: reconcile@reconcilinggodsway.org

FOCUS ON THE FAMILY®

Welcome to the Family

Whether you purchased this book, borrowed it, or received it as a gift, thanks for reading it! This is just one of many insightful, biblically based resources that Focus on the Family produces for people in all stages of life.

Focus is a global Christian ministry dedicated to helping families thrive as they celebrate and cultivate God's design for marriage and experience the adventure of parenthood. Our outreach exists to support individuals and families in the joys and challenges they face, and to equip and empower them to be the best they can be.

Through our many media outlets, we offer help and hope, promote moral values and share the life-changing message of Jesus Christ with people around the world.

Focus on the Family MAGAZINES

These faith-building, character-developing publications address the interests, issues, concerns, and challenges faced by every member of your family from preschool through the senior years.

For More INFORMATION

 ONLINE:
Log on to
FocusOnTheFamily.com
In Canada, log on to
FocusOnTheFamily.ca

 PHONE:
Call toll-free:
**800-A-FAMILY
(232-6459)**
In Canada, call toll-free:
800-661-9800

THRIVING FAMILY®	FOCUS ON	FOCUS ON	FOCUS ON
Marriage & Parenting	THE FAMILY CLUBHOUSE JR.® Ages 4 to 8	THE FAMILY CLUBHOUSE® Ages 8 to 12	THE FAMILY CITIZEN® U.S. news issues

Rev. 3/11

More Great Resources
from Focus on the Family®

***The Surprising Way to a Stronger Marriage:
How the Power of One Changes Everything***
by Michael and Amy Smalley
Surprise! You don't have to wait for a happier marriage.
You can make a difference, beginning today—by
changing yourself. Discover how the power of one
spouse, bolstered by the power of God and key principles from His Word, can change everything.

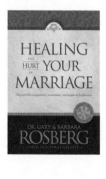

***Your Spouse Isn't the Person You Married:
Keeping Love Strong Through Life's Changes***
by Teri K. Reisser, MFT and Paul C. Reisser, MD
Using candid insights, humor, and stories drawn
from years of experience, the Reissers show how to
prevent and repair marriage rifts that develop with
time. Recapture intimacy and grow closer to your
spouse—not further apart.

***Healing the Hurt in Your Marriage:
Beyond Discouragement, Anger, and
Resentment to Forgiveness***
by Dr. Gary and Barbara Rosberg
Learn how to close the loop on unresolved conflict
through forgiveness. Dr. Gary and Barbara Rosberg
draw from biblical wisdom to offer a step-by-step
process that will move you beyond conflict to restore
hope, harmony, and intimacy in your marriage.

FOR MORE INFORMATION

 Online:
Log on to FocusOnTheFamily.com
In Canada, log on to FocusOnTheFamily.ca

 Phone:
Call toll-free: 800-A-FAMILY
In Canada, call toll-free: 800-661-9800

FOCUS®
ON THE FAMILY

BPZZXP1